Happy Birth...

Jane & Ross.

FROM THE LIBRARY OF

E. C. Izzard

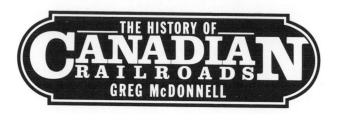

THE HISTORY OF
CANADIAN
RAILROADS
GREG McDONNELL

THE HISTORY OF
CANADIAN
RAILROADS
GREG McDONNELL

DEDICATION

For Maureen, who understood.
And for my mother, who inspired.
Come back Citizen Jane.

ACKNOWLEDGMENTS

As much as anything, this book is a work of the many photographers whose credit lines appear beneath each photo. A mere credit line is small compensation for the uncounted hours spent sorting through thousands of negatives and colour slides and for the meticulous darkroom work and generous provision of more than one thousand 8 × 10 prints and colour transparencies supplied for consideration. If this book has any one strong point, it is that its illustration has been provided by a group of this continent's finest railroad photographers. Many thanks to Messrs. Adeney, Begg, Brown and Cox; Drury, Hastings, Herbert and Hooper; More, Sanders and Sandusky; Shaughnessy and Shaw; Andrew and John Sutherland and Al Patterson and Dick George, curators of the Patterson-George Collection.

Special thanks are also in order to Walter Dressel, for Manitoba research; to the many archivists in Victoria, Ottawa, Montreal and Toronto for their assistance in the retrieval of older material; to Omer Lavallée, for his invaluable contribution of historical data relating to the Canadian Pacific and to Don McQueen for auditing the text.

Finally, thanks to my capable editor, Sheila Rosenzweig, without whom this book would not have been written.

Copyright © 1985 by Footnote Productions Limited

Exclusive to Coles
First published in Canada 1985 by New Burlington Books

ISBN 0 90628 663 8

Typeset by Central Southern Typesetters
Eastbourne, East Sussex, UK
Color separations by Hong Kong Scannercraft Company Ltd.
Printed by Leefung-Asco Printers Ltd.

This book was designed and produced by
Footnote Productions Ltd., 6 Blundell Street, London N6

Editorial Director: Sheila Rosenzweig
Art Director: Peter Bridgewater

1 2 3 4 5 6 7 8 9 0

CONTENTS

The first locomotive constructed in Canada was the *Toronto*, No. 2 of the Ontario, Simcoe & Huron Rail Road, later the Northern Railway of Canada. It was built by James Good in Toronto in 1853. The engine is pictured about 1880, just prior to scrapping. *CP Rail*

On Thursday, July 21, 1836, Canada — still a fledgling British colony 31 years short of confederation — joined the railway age. Towing a pair of passenger "carriages", an awkward-looking British-built 0–4–0 pulled away from the steamboat wharf at Laprairie, Quebec, and made a 14.5-mile-per-hour dash to St. Johns, Quebec, over the newly laid iron-strap rails of the Champlain & St. Lawrence Railroad. While several previous projects had employed horse-drawn rail cars and the construction of the Quebec Citadel in 1830 actually made use of a steam-driven cable car system to haul blocks of granite up a steep incline, the C.&St.L. is generally accepted as Canada's first railway.

THE CHAMPLAIN & ST. LAWRENCE RAILROAD

The C.&St.L. was constructed as a portage railway, although its actual function was as a short cut for New York–Montreal river traffic, rather than a true portage. Earlier, shipping followed a route up the Hudson River, Lake Champlain, Richelieu River and the St. Lawrence River. The C.&St.L. substituted a 14.5-mile St. Johns–Laprairie rail trip and a short Laprairie–Montreal ferry ride across the St. Lawrence for the previous 90-mile St. Johns–Sorel–Montreal route following the Richelieu and St. Lawrence rivers.

Promoters envisioned substantial freight business on the new railroad and posted rates for various commodities, including meats, flour and lumber, as early as three months prior to completion of the line. In spite of the reduction of transit time, shippers were discouraged by the exorbitant rates, and freight revenues were less than anticipated. Passengers, however, were not deterred by the seven shillings and sixpence excursion fare and they flocked to the railroad in throngs. Business boomed and the company paid dividends as high as 25 percent.

During the initial season, service on the C.&St.L. was provided by an 0–4–0 purchased from the English Newcastle-on-Tyne works of Robert Stephenson & Company for 1200 pounds sterling. Weighing in at "112 hundredweight, 0 quarters and 19 pounds" (12,563 pounds) and riding on four 48-inch wooden driving wheels, the *Dorchester* — as Canada's first steam locomotive was named — was an ungainly beast. Nevertheless, the *Dorchester* was capable of reaching speeds in excess of 30 miles per hour over the C.&St.L.'s rickety trackage and making the St. Johns–Laprairie trip in 41 minutes with as many as five cars.

Inexperience contributed to the growing pains that plagued the C.&St.L.'s early years. The primitive trackage, laid without ballast, and using wooden rails capped with three-inch-wide iron strapping, was unstable; the *Dorchester* suffered burned flues after its fireman let the boiler water run low, and the locomotive engineer provided by Stephenson & Company deserted the railway after several weeks. There are accounts of the train leaving Laprairie before the arrival of the ferry from Montreal; of unscheduled departures from St. Johns, and of passengers having to detrain and physically assist the train upgrade. On occasion, the iron-strap "rails" would break loose and slash through the floors of the railroad cars. And in spite of swinging gates installed at crossings, it took only until the summer of 1837 to record the first grade-crossing accident in Canada . . . at Côte St. Raphael, where the train derailed after striking a team of oxen.

These events were inconsequential, though, and the railroad continued to prosper, acquiring additional motive power. The *Jason C. Pierce*, a 4–2–0 built by William Norris of Philadelphia arrived in 1837. Over the next 15 years the C.&St.L. purchased eight 4–4–0s from Norris, Baldwin — also of Philadelphia — and from the Taunton Locomotive Works, of Taunton, Massachusetts, as well as buying the *John Molson*, a 2–2–2 built in 1847 by Kinmond Hutton and Steel, of Dundee, Scotland. The railroad extended its trackage 20 miles south to Rouses Point, New York, to connect with the Northern Railroad of New York. There are several replicas of the original *Dorchester* extant and a full-size, operational replica of the *John Molson* is at the Canadian Railway Museum at Delson, Quebec.

THE ALBION RAILWAY

The success of the Champlain & St. Lawrence inspired railway proposals from visionaries throughout the land, but while others were dreaming, Canada's second railway became a reality. An English jeweller, in possession of coal holdings once held by King George IV on the north shore of Nova Scotia, sponsored construction of the six-mile Albion Colliery Tramway (later the Albion Railway) opened in 1838. The Albion was constructed to move coal between the mines and Pictou Harbour. Though its role was less than glamorous, the Albion Railway was an impressive accomplishment, requiring more than 400,000 cubic yards of fill for embankments and incorporating bridges and culverts of cut stone as well as a 1500-foot shipping quay in the Pictou Harbour. A trio of British-built 0–6–0s were imported to work the coal trains and the line remained in operation for more than 50 years. When the road finally shut down, two of the Albion's 0–6–0s became the first Canadian beneficiaries of the steam preservation move-

ment. The *Samson*, one of the original trio built in 1838 by Timothy Hackworth, at New Shildar, Durham, England, and the *Albion*, built circa 1840, were saved from scrap, touring the continent on special flat cars for more than 30 years. After appearing at the Baltimore and Ohio's centennial celebrations in 1927, the two engines were donated to the province of Nova Scotia and returned "home." The *Samson* is displayed at New Glasgow, Nova Scotia, and the *Albion* is on display at Stellarton, in the same province.

THE EARLY SHORTLINES

Canadian railroading gained momentum through the late 1840s and early 1850s as shortlines began popping up everywhere. The first few were portage railways: the Montreal and Lachine, completed in 1847 between its namesake towns and regarded as operator of Canada's first commuter trains; and La Compagnie du Chemin à Rails du Saint-Laurent et du Village d'Industrie, a 12-mile line opened in 1850 between Lanorai on the St. Lawrence River and what is now the city of Joliette, Quebec. This road purchased the *Dorchester* and *Jason C. Pierce* (both converted to 2–4–0s years earlier) from the Champlain & St. Lawrence; and the Carillon & Grenville, begun in 1848 and finally opened on August 25, 1854.

The Carillon & Grenville holds the distinction of being the first Canadian railway to specify iron rails — boosting construction costs from £1200 to £6730 per mile — and is further distinguished as the last "broad gauge" (5′6″) railroad to operate on the continent. Although intended to form part of the proposed "Great Montreal and Ottawa Valley Trunk Line," the Carillon & Grenville was built as a true portage railway linking Ottawa River steamboat services separated by the unnavigable 12-mile-long Carillon Rapids. The C&G was orphaned when the ship carrying the railway's promoter, James Sykes, and £50,000 in cash to finance the GM&OVTL was lost at sea returning from England. The Carillon & Grenville lived on in isolation, allowing retention of its "broad" gauge, and the trains continued to meet Ottawa River steamboats until they were discontinued in 1910.

THE ST. LAWRENCE & ATLANTIC LINE

As early as 1834, a young man in Portland, Maine envisioned a railway linking Portland and Montreal. John A. Poor realized the advantages of such a route: a short cut to the Canadian interior and an ice-free port providing year-round outlet to England and Europe rather than the seasonal shipping on the St. Lawrence. It took 11 years of intensive, often

cut-throat politicking and promoting, but in 1845 Poor's dream was realized on both sides of the border, as the Atlantic & St. Lawrence in the United States and as the St. Lawrence & Atlantic in Canada.

Funding the $5 million project was difficult, but construction got under way after promoter Alexander Tilloch Galt returned from a fund-raising trip to England and the company located an American contractor willing to accept stock in the railroad as part payment. With completion of the first 30 miles — from Longueuil, Quebec (on the south shore of the

In one of the oldest known Canadian railway photographs, the *Samson*, built in England in 1838, poses with crew on Nova Scotia's Albion Railway. This engine has been preserved and is now on display at New Glasgow, N.S. *Public Archives Canada*

St. Lawrence, across from Montreal) to Ste. Hyacinthe — construction of the St. Lawrence & Atlantic Railroad ground to a halt. At the close of the year 1848, the company coffers had been tapped dry. However, by this time the St. Lawrence & Atlantic Railroad had political connections and legislation was soon passed authorizing government guarantees on the bonds of reputable railroads — those with at least 75 miles of trackage. The mileage restriction tied to the Railway Guarantee Act was the kicker. Galt pulled all the stops, mortgaging his holdings and selling stock — anything to bankroll extension of the St.L.&A. to Richmond, Quebec — which would give the line the necessary 75 miles of track.

The St.L.&A. reached Richmond in the fall of 1851, qualified for the government guarantees and pressed on for Island Pond, Vermont, and connection with its American counterpart, the Atlantic and St. Lawrence. By 1852 the St.L.&A./A.&St.L. was complete. Railway mania gripped the land. Canada — still 15 years away from confederation — was on the threshold of a political, social and technological revolution that would cast the die of her future.

FOUNDING THE GREAT WESTERN RAILWAY

In Canada West (now Ontario) ambitious plans — nurtured since the 1830s — were afoot to build a railway from the U.S. border at Niagara Falls to Windsor on the banks of the Detroit River and the Michigan border. The Great Western Railway would, its promoters boasted, tap the richest traffic potential in Canada as well as attracting U.S. bridge traffic over its short cut to the Midwest. In its day, the GWR would indeed be one of Canada's most efficient and prosperous railroads.

First sod was turned in a ceremony at London, Ontario, on October 23, 1849, but construction did not begin in earnest on the Great Western until 1851. The targetted completion date of December, 1852, came and went. The GWR was far behind schedule — racing time and the Toronto, Simcoe and Lake Huron, as well as the Buffalo, Brantford and Goderich (later the Buffalo and Lake Huron) in a scramble to be the first operational steam railroad in Canada West. The TS&LS Railway left the others behind, operating its first train from Toronto to Aurora on May 16, 1853. The Great Western continued to push toward completion,

paying little mind to quality.

The Niagara Falls–Hamilton section opened November 1, 1853, and the first Niagara Falls–London train ran on December 17 of that year. One week later, regular service commenced on the Windsor–Chatham segment, while crews worked feverishly to complete the gap between Chatham and London. On the eve of the first through train from Niagara Falls to Windsor, track crews worked all through the night laying the last rails by lantern light. The Great Western was officially opened on January 17, 1854, with the arrival in Windsor of two six-coach sections of the first through passenger train from Niagara Falls.

The GWR continued to build, extending a branch of the mainline from Hamilton to Toronto and stretching branchlines from Harrisburg to Galt (opened in 1854) and Komoka to Sarnia (opened in 1858). Later developments saw the GWR reach into the Bruce Peninsula, and attain Georgian Bay by assuming control of the Galt and Guelph Railway and the Wellington, Grey and Bruce lines. The GWR built the London, Huron and Bruce Railway as well, which opened in 1875 between London and Wingham.

Atlantic & St. Lawrence No. 6, a primitive, wooden-cabbed 4-4-0, poses with crew at an unknown location around 1856. *Canadian National photo*

Ornate Great Western 0–4–0 No. 82, the *William Weir*, stands outside what may be the Toronto, Ont. station in a photo believed to have been taken during the 1860s. *Canadian National photo*

For the next few years the Great Western paid the price of its hurried and haphazard construction. The frequency of serious accidents was alarming, with 19 accidents occurring in 1854 alone. Work trains completing construction crowded the line and interfered with regular trains. On October 27, 1854, a mail train collided with an unprotected ballast train near Chatham, Ontario, killing 52 persons, injuring 48, and prompting a government investigation of the conditions and operations of the GWR. Not surprisingly, the report was unfavourable, citing poor trackwork laid without ballast, unfinished road crossings and cattle guards, and generally substandard construction as well as incidents of negligent operations.

On March 12, 1857, in an occurrence unrelated to the GWR's teething pangs, the railroad suffered what remains one of the worst disasters in Canadian railroad history. A derailment, attributed to a broken wheel or axle on the lead truck of the locomotive *Oxford*, sent a Toronto–Hamilton express train plunging into the icy waters of the Desjardins Canal just outside of Hamilton. In a twist of irony, one of the 60 fatalities is said to have been the man responsible for the elimination of a prior mandatory stop at the approaches of the Desjardins bridge. Such a procedure would undoubtedly have prevented this accident or at least lessened the severity of the incident.

The task of upgrading the GWR was further complicated by the need to replace inferior rails used in the original construction. Only 34 miles of T-rail (the design is still in common use) were installed during the building of the Great Western, with the remaining miles consisting of 38 miles of compound rails and 156 miles of troublesome bridge rail. By the year 1860, improvements were under way. Eighty-two miles of compound and bridge rail had been replaced with T-rail and improvements to the physical plant were ongoing. However, an October report filed by the chief engineer forecast requirements for 3,000 tons of new rail, 836,000 ties and other improvements to be completed in a five-year period and at a cost of $2 million — five times the amount budgeted.

In spite of its problems, Great Western lived up to its potential, reaping the benefits of the industrial growth its presence spawned and attracting overhead or bridge traffic from connections established at Niagara Falls, Windsor and Sarnia. At Niagara Falls the GWR soared over the Niagara Gorge on an impressive suspension bridge that opened on March 19, 1855. Built by John A. Roebling, the famed American bridge builder whose credits include the Brooklyn Bridge, the GWR Suspension Bridge facilitated interchange with the standard-gauge Rochester, Lockport & Niagara Falls Railroad (which became part of the New

York Central) and the six-foot gauge Elmira, Canandaigua and Niagara Falls Railway. Car ferries across the Detroit River at Windsor and the St. Clair River at Sarnia made connections with U.S. roads at Detroit and Port Huron respectively.

Incorporation of the Erie & Niagara Extension Railway (renamed the Canada Southern before construction began), chartered in 1869 to build from Fort Erie to Amherstburg, posed a serious threat to GWR's lucrative international traffic. The Great Western responded with the Canada Air Line Railway to be built from the mainline at Glencoe to Canfield,

The Great Western's Glencoe–Welland Junction, Ont. Canada Airline Railway was still under construction in 1872 when GWR 4-4-0 No. 7, along with a work train and construction gang, paused for the photographer on the recently completed trestle over Catfish Creek, near St. Thomas. *Ontario Archives*

where trackage rights over the Buffalo and Lake Huron would bring trains to Fort Erie and Buffalo. The purpose of the Air Line was threefold: to expedite international traffic; to counteract the threat of the CASO; and to eliminate the need to double-track the congested London–Windsor mainline.

With the Canada Southern and the Great Western in a high-stakes race to completion, the Grand Trunk thwarted the GWR's plans, gaining control of the Buffalo and Lake Huron and prohibiting Great Western running rights. This move forced Great Western to extend the Air Line an additional 45 miles to Welland

Junction, to purchase running rights over the Welland Railway to Port Robinson, and to build the nine-mile Allenburg Spur into Niagara Falls. The delay stalled completion by one year and cost the company dearly. Through service on the Canada Southern commenced in November, 1873, while the Air Line did not open until December 15.

Through the years, the Great Western racked up a number of firsts and notable accomplishments. The company's Hamilton shops turned out the first sleeping cars in the land in 1857–1858 and followed in 1861 with the nation's first steel-boilered locomotive, a

Sporting headlights front and rear, GWR 0–4–2T No. 208, built in Philadelphia in 1872, is an unkempt example of Great Western yard power.
Canadian National photo

home-built 0–6–0 named the *Scotia*. The Great Western also lays claim to Canada's first on-train mail sorting, introduced in 1854; the first iron-hulled ice-breaking car ferry — placed in service between Windsor and Detroit in January, 1867; and GWR holds the dubious distinction of being the intended victim in North America's first attempted train robbery. On June 27, 1856, an alert track inspector (wounded for his efforts) foiled the plans of two men who removed a rail from the mainline near Mosa Station (some 33 miles west of London) with the intention of derailing and robbing a GWR passsenger train.

PROVINCIAL GAUGE LEGISLATION

Along with its arch-rival the Grand Trunk, a great thorn in the side of GWR was the 5'6″ Provincial Gauge made mandatory by the government in 1851. This broad gauge — forced upon the Great Western — made direct interchange with standard gauge (4'8½″) U.S. roads impossible and necessitated transshipment of all through freight at both ends. In 1864, the GWR struck a compromise solution, dual-gauging the entire Niagara Falls–Windsor mainline and later the Sarnia branch.

By laying a third rail inside the broad gauge, the GWR could handle standard and broad gauge cars. Trains handling standard-gauge consists were identified by a large N.G. displayed on the front of the engine.

The Provincial Gauge legislation was finally repealed in 1870. The Great Western's response was dramatic: the entire Hamilton–Toronto line was standard-gauged in eight hours on one day in December, 1870. It took several months to convert the mainline and the entire railroad was standard gauge by June, 1873.

THE FALL OF THE GWR

The elimination of provincial gauge simplified life for the Great Western, although the other thorn in its side — the Grand Trunk — continued to harass the GWR. Competition between the two railroads heated up and rate wars ensued. In the early 1880s, rumblings that the Canadian Pacific Railway was eyeing the GWR as a means of expansion in the east spurred the Grand Trunk to action. The GTR put forth proposals to merge, lease or take over the Great Western, but the offers were rejected. Its friendly overtures spurned, the Grand Trunk

began collecting GWR proxies and with less than one percent interest managed to force a special meeting of the stockholders. The Grand Trunk rammed through its takeover bid. On August 12, 1882, the 852-mile Great Western Railway was absorbed by the Grand Trunk.

THE GRAND TRUNK

In both name and purpose, inspiration for the Grand Trunk Railway was found in the trunk roads of Imperial Rome. Indeed, those who initiated plans for the Canadian Main

Great Western Railway broad-gauge 2–4–0 *Oberon* displays the mandatory NG plate, indicating a consist of standard, or "narrow" gauge cars.

Line that would become the Grand Trunk envisioned it as a government-owned project, sponsored by the Imperial government in England to bind and unite the colonies of British North America (as pre-confederation Canada was known). The original proposal to build from Halifax to the western boundary of Canada West lost out to the routing preferred by influential politicians in the colonies who saw the railroad as a vehicle to build personal empires. On November 10, 1852, the Grand Trunk Railway was incorporated to build from Montreal to Toronto. An anxious Canadian government quickly passed legislation extending the Grand Trunk west to Sarnia and east to Portland, Maine, with additional provisions for a line to be built to New Brunswick as a link with the proposed Intercolonial Railway to Halifax, and a loop line from Belleville through Peterborough to Toronto.

Imperialistic from the start, the Grand Trunk's plan of action was to purchase existing railways and charters along the Portland–Sarnia route, then simply to fill in the gaps.

Plans to incorporate the Great Western as the mainline west of Toronto were dropped when the GWR held out for a price beyond what the GTR was prepared to pay, setting the stage for some of the most vicious competition in Canadian railroad history. The story of Grand Trunk's formative years is a twisted tale of corruption and swindles, of politics, high finance and mismanagement. Construction costs quickly soared high above the estimated £8,000 per mile and promotors misrepresented the state of completed railways to be absorbed.

When plans to take over the St. Lawrence and Atlantic and the Atlantic and St. Lawrence as the GTR's Montreal-to-Portland route were formulated, promotors billed the road as operational and forecast an immediate annual surplus of £100,000. In reality, the railroad was in terrible condition: roadbeds were unstable, trackage unballasted, grades too steep and stations and other support facilities were either incomplete or nonexistant. It cost the Grand Trunk £850,000 just to make the line operational and even then, it was not yet safe

First of scores of engines to wear the "built in GTR shops" label, Grand Trunk 4–4–0 No. 209, the *Trevithick*, was turned out of the company's Pointe St. Charles Shops in Montreal in May 1859. *Canadian National photo*

for trains to run at night. Within a year, ballasting was nearly complete and trains were making the 292-mile Longueuil-to-Portland journey (across the St. Lawrence from Montreal) in 11½ hours, achieving an average speed of 26 miles per hour. The Richmond–Lévis section of the Maritime connection and the Toronto–Oshawa line were opened by the fall of 1855; the Toronto–Sarnia mainline was opened as far as Guelph (48 miles) by July, 1856 and on October 26, 1856, a seven-car passenger train opened the Toronto–Montreal line.

INTRODUCTION OF THE BIRKENHEADS

In conjunction with the construction of the Grand Trunk — an undertaking of unprecedented magnitude (in Canada) — the contractors built the Canada Works at Birkenhead, England to manufacture GTR locomotives, cars and bridge parts. Between 1854 and 1858, the Grand Trunk took delivery of 50 Birken-

head locomotives, shipped across the Atlantic in a specially equipped vessel owned by the Canada Works. The Birkenheads were a hybrid creature combining the characteristics of contemporary British and American locomotives. Cosmetically, they were clumsy-looking, with American-style balloon stacks and large wooden cowcatchers that clashed with their small British headlamps and side-mounted sand boxes — but the Birkenheads quickly earned a reputation as powerful brutes, reliable and nearly indestructable.

Early Birkenheads were built as 2–4–0s and took a beating on the rough GTR trackage until converted to the 4–4–0 American Standard configuration adopted by later arrivals.

American Standards of diversified origin, including hand-me-down Portland-built engines inherited from the St.L.&A., Kinmonds (including the second locomotive built in Canada) from the Montreal works of Kinmond Bros. opened in 1852, 51 (by 1866) from the Canadian Engine & Machine Co. of Kingston, Ontario (CLC) and 25 diamond-stacked 4–4–0s built by Nielson and Co. in 1868 dominated the Grand Trunk roster in the early years. Company-built locomotives from the Grand Trunk's Pointe St. Charles shops in Montreal were added to the fleet beginning with 4–4–0 No. 209, the *Trevithick,* outshopped in May, 1859. From a stable of 34 locomotives in 1853, the Grand Trunk roster swelled to over 325 engines by 1870, when total locomotive mileage averaged 642,772 miles per month.

BRIDGING THE ST. LAWRENCE

One of the most formidable obstacles facing the Grand Trunk was bridging the St. Lawrence River at Montreal. Engineers of the day claimed construction of a two-mile long bridge over the rapid-running St. Lawrence waters at a location prone to flooding and severe ice jams would be sheer lunacy. Nevertheless, in September, 1854, a contract for such a bridge was let to Peto, Brassey, Jackson & Betts — the contractors responsible for the Toronto–Montreal and Richmond–Lèvis line.

It was estimated that the bridge would take from five to six years to build, forcing the GTR to find an interim solution. A trio of 167-foot-long ferries carried passengers and cargo between Montreal and the south shore, while rolling stock was moved over the river on barges towed by tugs. In winter, passengers and freight were towed across the river ice on sleds.

The first caisson was floated into place on May 24, 1854. During the next five years and five months, an army of labourers, rivermen, stonemasons, smiths, carpenters and ironworkers — nearly 3,000 in number — laboured

year round, through the insufferable heat of summer and the cruel cold of winter. Stone — more than 70,000 tons of it cut from quarries 16 miles upstream — was floated to the site by tugs and river barges while the tubular superstructure was shipped from the Canada Works at Birkenhead. The rectangular superstructure consisted of 25 tubular spans with plate girder sides and a tin-sheathed wooden roof. The tubes were constructed in pairs, connected with expansion joints and mounted on rollers. So precise was Birkenhead's prefabrication of the ironwork that not one of the 1,540,000 rivet holes had to be reamed or redrilled.

During 1859, the GTR offered contractors an additional £300,000 if the bridge could be completed before year's end. By September, the substructure was complete. On December 15, 1859, a triple-headed 18-car trainload of stone (double the weight of an average train) successfully tested the structure in the presence of the inspector of railroads. On December 17, the 10,410-foot–long Victoria Tubular Bridge opened for regular traffic. On August 25, 1860, HRH the Prince of Wales (later crowned King Edward VII) drove the final rivet in place in a ceremony formally completing the bridge.

The Guelph–Sarnia section of the mainline was opened November 21, 1859, and completion of the Victoria Bridge made possible continuous rail travel between the Michigan boundary and the Atlantic Ocean. The dreams of a Canadian mainline (as well as the dreams of John Poor) were finally fulfilled.

The Victoria Tubular Bridge remained in use until 1898, when the double-tracked Victoria Jubilee Bridge, constructed around the tubular bridge without significant inter-

ruption of traffic, was opened. This bridge remains in use today, carrying Canadian National Railway's mainline east of Montreal, as well as highway vehicular traffic on separate roadways flanking the tracks.

DISASTER ON THE RICHELIEU RIVER BRIDGE

The Victoria Bridge brought fame to the Grand Trunk, but the bridge over the Richelieu River at Beloeil, Quebec (only about 15 miles to the east) brought the railroad infamy. On June 28, 1864, a special GTR passenger train with 354 German immigrants aboard left Lèvis, Quebec, for Montreal. The westbound special with 4–4–0 No. 168 HAM (built by D. C. Gunn at Hamilton, Ontario), two baggage cars, seven produce cars temporarily outfitted for passenger service, a second-class coach and a brake van (caboose), arrived at the intermediate division point of Richmond, Quebec, after all available engine crews had departed with previous specials. In spite of the fact that the incoming engineer had never run an engine west of Richmond, he was persuaded to take the train to Montreal with a new crew.

The train, approaching Beloeil in unfamiliar territory, sped past the mandatory stop at the east end of the Richelieu River Bridge, failed to observe the signals indicating an open drawbridge and at 1:15 A.M., June 29, 1864, plunged through the open draw and crashed onto a passing barge. In the aftermath, the train lay at the bottom of the river. Its wreckage was piled high on the barge and 99 people were dead. This remains Canada's worst railroad accident.

STANDARD GAUGING THE GRAND TRUNK

Just as it did with the Great Western, the 5'6" Provincial Gauge frustrated the Grand Trunk's efforts to boost profitable American interchange and overhead traffic. While the Great Western went dual-gauge, the Grand Trunk opted for a unique solution.

In 1869, the GTR introduced adjustable-gauge freight car trucks featuring telescoping axles, normally locked in position, but capable of changing gauge when unlocked and run through a short stretch of tapering track. Cars fitted with the new truck were assigned to Chicago–Boston through service, with shippers paying a premium for reduced transit time. The GTR reaped savings through elimination of trans-shipment of freight and reduced damage claims. So great was the demand for the new cars that the GTR and several connecting roads — including Michigan Central and the Vermont Central — contracted with the National Despatch Car Company to supply a fleet of adjustable-trucked pool cars that eventually numbered 1,300 cars.

However popular, the trucks were not completely successful. They had a tendency to slip out of gauge at inopportune moments, this being responsible for a number of derailments. As a result, the GTR adopted a practice of exchanging standard for broad-gauge trucks on cars received in interchange and reversing the procedure on cars being returned.

The ultimate solution to the problem was conversion to standard gauge, a programme the Grand Trunk began in 1872. In a direct attempt to better compete with the Great Western, the Sarnia–Fort Erie route (which included part of the Buffalo & Lake Huron acquired years earlier) was narrowed to standard gauge on Sunday, November 17, and

Top Left: The worst railway accident in Canadian history occurred at 1:15 A.M. June 29, 1864, when a Grand Trunk passenger special plunged through an open draw on the Richelieu River bridge at Beloiel, Quebec, crashing on to a passing barge and killing 99 persons. In the aftermath of the incident, rescue workers inspect the wreckage, which remains piled upon the barge. Public Archives Canada

Bottom: Beginning in 1874, the Grand Trunk operated a succession of steam-powered "dummies" between Bridgeburg (Fort Erie), Ont. and Black Rock (Buffalo), N.Y. Canadian National photo

Monday, November 18, 1872. A few days prior to the overnight transformation, several locomotives and a small fleet of cars were converted to standard gauge and readied for immediate service on the new line. The remaining trackage west of Toronto was converted in October, 1873, and during the following month the Toronto–Montreal–Portland line was done. The Richmond–Lèvis–Rivière du Loup branch was finally standard-gauged in 1874.

Standard-gauging a system the size of the Grand Trunk presented the company with a challenge of unprecedented magnitude. On the mainline, 10-man gangs were assigned every 2½ miles; extra gangs handled yards, sidings and roundhouses. Shop crews (paid an incentive of time-and-a-half for each shift worked) performed around the clock converting locomotives and rolling stock. Many older engines were simply retired or sold and replaced by more efficient power — including 0–4–0Ts from Baldwin and 4–4–0s from Manchester, Rhode Island and Portland. As the GTR purged itself of unwanted broad-gauge engines, smaller lines and industries picked up bargain-priced locomotives, many of which survived in the backwoods of Quebec and New Brunswick until the turn of the century.

EXPANSION OF THE GTR

From its inception, the Grand Trunk maintained an expansionist policy. This Canadian giant voraciously gobbled up competition and connections, large or small, rich or poor. After assuming control of the Montreal–Portland, St.L.&A. and A.&St.L., the GTR's next significant acquisition was the Montreal & Champlain, an amalgamation that included Canada's first railway — the Champlain & St. Lawrence. In 1850, the C.&St.L. purchased the St. Johns, Quebec–Rouses Point, N.Y., Montreal and Province Line Junction Railway and established connecting service with the Northern Railroad of New York (later the Ogdensburg & Lake Champlain Railroad). Two years later, the Montreal & Lachine merged with the Lake St. Louis & Province Line Railroad running from Caughnawaga (on the south shore opposite Montreal) to the U.S. border just north of Mooers, N.Y. A fierce rivalry raged unchecked until June 1862, when the two roads merged as the Montreal & Champlain. On the verge of bankruptcy, the M&C was taken over by the Grand Trunk on September 25, 1863.

One of the primary motives behind GTR's acquisition of the standard gauge M&C was to gain access to the ex-Montreal & Lachine's Bonaventure Station in Montreal. The GTR quickly facilitated the move, constructing a connecting track between its own mainline and the former M&L as well as dual-gauging the

newly acquired Montreal trackage. In addition, a connection with the M&C was established at St. Lambert and a third rail laid across the Victoria Bridge to allow M&C trains to reach Bonaventure Station.

During 1873, at the height of its campaign to convert to standard gauge, the GTR temporarily suspended all service on the Caughnawaga–Mooers Jct. "Caughnawaga Division" of the M&C and used the line to store new standard-gauge locomotives and cars. Enraged at the total loss of service, local citizens removed the stored equipment.

Striking a traditional pose at the Meaford, Ont. station are Northern Railway 4–4–0 No. 3, coach 24, passengers and crew. *Public Archives Canada*

THE INTERNATIONAL BRIDGE

The Buffalo & Lake Huron, a struggling Goderich–Brantford–Fort Erie branchline — already spurned by the Great Western — was added to the Grand Trunk fold in 1864. Although the north end of the line offered few immediate prospects, the potential of a gateway to the United States at Fort Erie/Buffalo was inviting. Car ferry service was established on the Niagara River between Fort Erie and Buffalo and in 1870, construction began on the International Bridge linking the two points.

Bad weather, strong Niagara currents, difficulties in locating solid footings for some of the ten bridge piers, and collisions between stationary caissons and passing timber rafts delayed completion for nearly a year. Finally, on October 27, 1873, the 3,624-foot International Bridge opened to traffic. By mid-November, the Canada Southern was exercising rights over the bridge and in September 1874, the GTR inaugurated an international passenger shuttle, using a self-propelled, steam-powered dummy.

The establishment of the Port Huron/Sarnia–Fort Erie/Buffalo bridge route doubled the American transit traffic within several years and turned the once unwanted Buffalo & Lake Huron into a vital artery.

Spurred by the success of the Buffalo & Lake Huron acquisition, the Grand Trunk cast an aggressive eye toward the maze of marginal feeder lines spread throughout southwestern Ontario. That the Great Western was already firmly entrenched in the Bruce Peninsula — with control of the Wellington, Grey and Bruce and the London, Bruce and Huron — lent a sense of urgency to the matter.

The GTR went shopping and in March, 1881, amassed its new-found holdings under the umbrella of the Grand Trunk, Georgian Bay and Lake Erie Railway Company, a wholly owned subsidiary. Included in the GT,GB&LE was the Port Dover and Lake Huron which ran cross-country from Port Dover on Lake Erie, to Stratford; its intended merger mate, the Stratford & Huron — its drive north to

Although still wearing Midland Railway identification in this photo dated Lindsay, Ont. 1890, 4-4-0 No. 605 and the accompanying coach, as well as the Midland itself, are the property of the Grand Trunk — as evidenced on the caboose just right of the 605. *Public Archives Canada*

Wiarton, on the west shore of Georgian Bay, stalled at Harriston — and the Georgian Bay and Wellington Railway, building between Palmerston and Durham. The branch to Durham opened November 7, 1881, and the Stratford & Huron finally reached Wiarton on November 29.

By now wary of the Canadian Pacific intrusions in the east, the Grand Trunk pulled off a defensive masterstroke resulting in the takeover of the entire Great Western — along with its U.S. property, the Detroit, Grand Haven & Milwaukee, a 191-mile line between Detroit and Grand Haven, Michigan, with a car ferry across Lake Michigan to Milwaukee. This gave the GTR a near stranglehold on southwestern Ontario and swelled the company to the seventh-largest railroad in North America.

ACQUISITION OF THE MIDLAND RAILWAY

On a roll and doing its utmost to block the CPR, the GTR flexed its muscles again in 1884. The Grank Trunk took control of the Midland Railway, a central Ontario interest that had itself absorbed a clutch of regional shortlines and spun a 469-mile web of branchlines extending from Belleville in the east, as far north as Haliburton and west to Midland on the shores of Georgian Bay.

The Midland's origins trace back to the ambitious and profitable Port Hope, Lindsay and Beaverton Railway Company, opened between Port Hope and Lindsay on December 30, 1857, with the branch to Peterborough completed May 12, 1858. One of the most prosperous shortlines in Canada, the PHL&B changed its name to the Midland Railway in 1869, and embarked on its expansionist career. The Peterborough branch was lengthened 9.5 miles to reach Lakefield in 1870 and in 1871 the push toward Georgian Bay saw the mainline extended to Beaverton. Problems with the original contract — let to Walter Stanley, of Hoosac Tunnel fame — delayed completion of the 59 miles between Beaverton and Midland until 1879. The Midland then sought to satisfy its appetite for expansion by absorbing neighbouring shortlines. From their Peterborough headquarters (moved from Port Hope in 1878) the Midland directors engineered a series of takeovers (believed to be backed by the GTR) that would triple the road's mileage.

The first to fall was the 64-mile Grand Junction Railway, built from Belleville to Peterborough on the revived charter of Grand Trunk's still-born Loop-line but with its sights set on Georgian Bay. Next in line was the former narrow-gauge Scarborough–Coboconk, Toronto & Nipissing Railway acquired along with its connecting Stouffville–Sutton subsidiary, the Lake Simcoe Junction Railway.

Other victims included: the Victoria Railway, running from Lindsay to Haliburton; the Belleville & North Hastings Railway, a short arm of the Grand Junction; the 22-mile Whitby, Port Perry & Lindsay; and the Toronto & Ottawa Railway, an unbuilt charter, used only to build three short connections totalling 29 miles.

Excluded from the Midland collection was one of the earliest and most colourful railways chartered in Upper Canada, an unfortunate outfit known as the Cobourg and Peterborough Railway. Completed between its namesake towns on December 29, 1854, the railroad was forced to close for the winter when its ramshackle wooden trestle across Rice Lake was damaged by ice jams. Reopened in the spring, the C&P led an impoverished existence that changed from bad to worse when in 1858 the Port Hope, Lindsay and Beaverton (eventually the original Midland Railway) reached Peterborough and siphoned off most of the area's business.

For a time the struggling C&P had to dodge bailiffs holding writs of seizure. G. R. Steven's CNR history recounts the tale of a Northumberland County sheriff who boarded the last coach of the Peterborough train at Cobourg, intent upon serving such a writ at Harwood. The sheriff was outfoxed by the train's conductor who, aware of the situation, uncoupled the coach at the crest of a grade north of Cobourg and let it coast back to town. Undaunted, the sheriff attempted to race the train to Rice Lake, arriving by horse and buggy in time to discover that all moveable company possessions had been loaded aboard the train and taken to Peterborough County — outside his jurisdiction.

Ice jams again piled up against the delicate Rice Lake trestle in the spring of 1860 and subsequent passage over the structure was of questionable safety. For some unknown reason, the Prince of Wales included the Cobourg and Peterborough on the itinerary of his visit in the fall of 1860. Rather than place the royal visitor at risk, the C&P hired a steamboat to sail the Prince across Rice Lake. In keeping with the luck of the C&P, the steamer experienced boiler trouble on the appointed day and His Royal Highness was rowed — in inclement weather — across the rough waters of Rice Lake while his train crept gingerly over the trestle.

The winter ice of 1860–1861 dealt the final blow to the Rice Lake bridge, assisted, it is said, by several men hired by the rival PH,L&B to remove strategically located bolts.

A briefly successful branch of the C&P to ore mines established at Blairton was opened in 1867 and shut down in 1883. The company was passed on to the Grand Trunk in 1893. The Cobourg–Rice Lake section was abandoned in

Top: Still sporting link-and-pin couplers in this June 1893 view (but trailing a tender), a St. Clair Tunnel Co. 0–10–0 Camelback exits the tunnel at Sarnia, with the "Atlantic Express" enveloped in dangerous exhaust and smoke gasses. *Public Archives Canada*

Bottom: The rationale for tunnel electrification is evidenced as a pair of St.CTCo. boxcab electrics, successors of the smoky 0–10–0's, make a clean escape from the St. Clair Tunnel with an eastbound passenger train. *Canadian National photo*

23

1895 and the Rice Lake–Peterborough line was torn up during the scrap-metal drives of World War I.

The Grand Trunk struck yet another coup on January 24, 1888, with the acquisition of the 492–mile "system" jointly operated by one-time rivals, the Northern Railway and the Hamilton & North Western. Tracing its roots to the Toronto, Simcoe & Lake Huron Railway, the Northern Railway holdings included: the original Toronto–Collingwood line; the North Simcoe Railway built from the TS&LH connection at Colwell to Penetanguishene; the Toronto, Simcoe & Muskoka Junction Railway from Barrie to Gravenhurst and the North Grey Railway, an extension of the TS&LH, built along the shore of Nottawasaga Bay from Collingwood to Meaford. The Grand Trunk's junior partner, the Hamilton and North Western, consisted of the former Hamilton & Lake Erie line between Hamilton and Port Dover, as well as the Hamilton & North Western "proper," built from Hamilton to Barrie with a branch from Allimill to Collingwood. Also included in the transaction was the jointly sponsored 111-mile Northern and Pacific Junction Railway, built from Gravenhurst to Callendar in the hopes of connecting with the Canadian Pacific's transcontinental mainline. The N&P Jct. was completed in 1886, but Canadian Pacific refused to interchange with the new arrival. Brief thoughts of extending westward to Sault Ste. Marie were entertained but sanity prevailed and the partnership surrendered regretfully to the Grand Trunk takeover.

International boundaries could not restrain the Grand Trunk's expansionist policies. Even before the mainline reached Sarnia, the GTR sponsored the building of, and then leased, the Chicago, Detroit and Canada Grand Trunk Junction Railroad from Port Huron to Detroit. St. Clair River car ferries connected the two lines and the tiny 60-mile U.S. line fed the GTR traffic faster than the ferries could handle it. Backlogs of as many as 700 cars have been recorded and flour traffic alone totalled 30,000 barrels per week. According to the Grand Trunk, traffic was limited only by the availability of rolling stock. Applying the same techniques it had employed elsewhere, the Grand Trunk established a sizable Michigan network by simply taking over fledgling shortlines.

In 1880, the GTR achieved the ultimate victory — a mainline slicing through Michigan across the top of Indiana and into Chicago. The road to Chicago had not been easy, however; en route, the GTR had to cleverly out-manoeuvre William Vanderbilt to gain possession of key trackage. The attempts to cross Vanderbilt's North Shore, Michigan Southern and Rock Island Railroad on the final approach to Chicago were met with violence. Engines were

derailed, trackage ripped up, fires set and near-rioting ensued before the confrontation was ended and the GTR — fondly embraced as the "giant killer" — took Chicago.

By 1890, Grand Trunk possessions west of the Canadian border included: the original Chicago, Detroit and Canada Grand Trunk Junction Railway; the Michigan Air Line Railway built from CD&DGT Jct. at Richmond, through Pontiac to Jackson, Michigan; the Cincinnati Saginaw and Mackinaw from the mainline at Durand, Michigan, to Saginaw and Bay City, Michigan; the Toledo, Saginaw and Muskegon, an isolated branch from Ashley to Muskegon, reached via Owosso–Ashley trackage rights over the Toledo, Ann Arbor and North Michigan; the Detroit, Grand Haven and Milwaukee Railway, with its Lake Michigan car ferry and the mainline, which ran west from Port Huron to Chicago and included a short branch to Kalamazoo.

To threatened CPR advances into New England the Grand Trunk responded with defensive action that culminated in control of the Central Vermont, gained in 1885. This gave the GTR some additional trackage in Southern Quebec, but more important, it created a second New England mainline, this one through Vermont (with branches to Richmond and Burlington) to the Atlantic port of New London, Connecticut.

During the same period the Grand Trunk reached into upper New York state with a line from Brosseau, Quebec (on the former M&C, near St. Lambert) to Massena, New York, where it connected with the Rome, Watertown and Ogdensburg Railroad — later to become part of the New York Central.

From an 8 × 10 glass plate negative, a company photo of a grimy but rare GTR 4–4–2T. Built at Pointe St. Charles Shops in 1882, Grand Trunk No. 1532 became CNR No. 43 and survived until 1934. *Canadian National photo*

THE ST. CLAIR TUNNEL

Boasting a single-line routing between Chicago and the Atlantic seaboard, the Grand Trunk quickly became a contender in the intense competition for traffic between the American Midwest and New England. Indeed, by 1883 the Grand Trunk carried one-third of all Chicago–New England traffic. However, the more bridge traffic the GTR won over, the greater the congestion became at the St. Clair River ferry slips. In the early 1880s time-sensitive dressed meat traffic reached record levels and the time had come to deal with the railroad's Achilles' heel once and for all. Heavy shipping on the St. Clair River prohibited construction of a bridge and test-boring conducted in 1885 revealed the same heavy blue clay that had defeated the Michigan Central's attempts to dig a Detroit–Windsor tunnel in 1872. Undaunted, the GTR persevered with the project and after considerable investigation determined that shield tunnelling — a recent innovation in tunnelling technology — could get the job done.

After an unsuccessful start in the spring of 1888, work finally got underway in January 1889. Rammed through the stiff blue clay from both sides of the border, the two 21-foot–diameter shields met in exact alignment some 80 feet below the surface of the St. Clair River on August 30, 1890. On September 19, the 6,000-foot–long, $2.7 million St. Clair tunnel saw its first train. The tunnel slashed two hours from the schedules of through trains, saved $50,000 per year over the ferry operations and gave the GTR a competitive edge that would go unchallenged until 1910, when Michigan

Central opened the Detroit River tunnel between Detroit and Windsor.

The St. Clair Tunnel Company commissioned four mammoth 0–10–0T Baldwin Camelbacks (the largest locomotives in the world upon their completion) for service through the tunnel. And for the next 18 years moving tonnage under the St. Clair River was a hazardous and dirty job. Crews endured smoke and hot gasses as the massive, 10-coupled Baldwins laboured up the 2 percent grades exiting the tunnel.

The dangerous steam-powered tunnel operation was made workable through safety precautions — placing cabooses directly behind the engines; operating all trains without air-brakes (a break-in-two would stall a train in the gas-filled tunnel); and instructions warning firemen not to put "green" coal on the fire while

Grand Trunk 4–4–0 No. 505 rolls into an unidentified Western Ontario station with a one-car passenger train. *Canadian National photo*

Canada Atlantic Baldwin 4–4–0 No. 15 stands at CAR's Elgin Street yards in Ottawa, Ont. during the 1890s. No. 15 would become GTR No. 1322 after 1905, then GTR No. 2121 and finally CN No. 246 before being scrapped in December 1924. *Public Archives Canada*

working through the tunnel. All the same, the inevitable accident occurred after only three years. Somewhere in the tunnel, heavy slack action parted the consist of an international freight train. But there were no train-line air-brakes to throw the train into an emergency stop and the caboose was coupled immediately behind engine 599. The entire crew emerged from the tunnel unscathed, with the first half of the train. At St. Clair, adherence to the operating rules had averted disaster ... temporarily. Apparently under pressure to retrieve the second half of the train, the crew returned to the tunnel without waiting for the gasses to clear and were quickly overcome. A six-man rescue party, dispatched after the 599 failed to return, was also overcome. A second rescue party managed to pull the 11 trapped men clear, but for the 599's engineer, conductor and brakemen, it was too late.

Talk of electrifying the line through the tunnel was not taken seriously until a second accident in 1903 asphyxiated several more men. On May 17, 1908, six 750 hp Baldwin–Westinghouse boxcab-electrics (later joined by three more BW electrics) banished steam from the tunnel. During their tunnel careers the four 0–10–0s had been converted to tender engines and renumbered from 598–601 to 1301–1304. After the electrics took over the big Baldwins were bumped into yard service, converted from camelback to the standard cab-in-rear configuration, and survived until the early 1920s as GT Nos. 2650–2653.

The highly regarded St. Clair tunnel project was by no means the only major improvement undertaken by the Grand Trunk during the close of the 19th century. The GTR was coming of age. During the late 1800s and into the early years of the 20th century the company embarked on a number of ambitious undertakings that saw the double-tracking of the entire

mainline from Ste. Rosalie, Quebec to Chicago, Illinois (with the exception of the passage through the St. Clair tunnel) as well as the line from Hamilton to Suspension Bridge. At the same time, mainline gradients were reduced; old 56- and 65-pound rail was replaced with 80–100 pound-per-yard rail. Nearly every mainline bridge was replaced, including the Victoria, Suspension and International bridges at Montreal, Niagara Falls and Fort Erie, respectively. Furthermore, the company shops were modernized and upgraded along with the motive power fleets they maintained.

CHANGING MOTIVE POWER

Although its popularity was on a downward swing, the GTR maintained its long-standing commitment to the standard type 4–4–0. As late as 1899 the company took delivery of multitudes of the eight-wheelers, from no less than ten builders, as well as the company shops. The Grand Trunk adapted the 4–4–0 to suit almost every imaginable service and still rostered an astounding count of 131 of these engines when absorbed by the CNR. In spite of its fondness for the 4–4–0, the GTR realized its limitations and by 1880 the company's Pointe St. Charles shops were turning out 2–6–0s. The Mogul type quickly succeeded the 4–4–0 as the Grand Trunk's engine for the future. Literally hundreds of 2–6–0s were acquired from American manufacturers (Rhode Island, Brooks, Dickson, Schenectady and Baldwin) and Canadian builders (Kingston and Montreal) as well as from Pte. St. Charles shops and those of the Chicago and Grand Trunk at Battle Creek, Michigan. The GTR continued to acquire 2–6–0s until 1910 and had 378 on hand when CNR took over. Coupled with physical improvements made over much of the system,

the new power nearly doubled the number of loaded cars per train in many areas.

The balance of GTR's turn-of-the-century roster was filled out by rare 0–4–0Ts and 4–4–2Ts; company-built 0–6–0Ts; and commercially built 0–6–0s as well as a handful of 4–6–0s. While much of this power survived well into the 1930s or later, there are few survivors today. Among those fortunate enough to escape the torch are an 0–6–0T built at Pte. St. Charles in 1894 and a 2–6–0 built at PSC in 1900. By far the oldest existing Grand Trunk engine is a 4–4–0 No. 40, built at Portland in 1872, part of one of the company's first orders for standard gauge locomotives. All three of these engines were part of the CNR's "Museum Train" and are now preserved at the Museum of Science and Technology, in Ottawa, Ontario.

ACQUIRING THE CANADA ATLANTIC RAILWAY

While the Grand Trunk continued to refine its physical plant and upgrade its locomotive fleet — ultimately acquiring a stable of 4–6–2s and 2–8–2s — the railroad engaged in one final act of aggression. In 1905, the Grand Trunk purchased the 396.6-mile Canada Atlantic Railway from lumber baron J. R. Booth. Stretching from a junction with the Central Vermont at East Alburgh, Vermont, to the Georgian Bay port of Depot Harbour, Ontario, the Canada Atlantic formed the shortest route between New England and the upper Great Lakes. The Grand Trunk bid of $14 million was high enough to shut out CAR's less-formidable suitors, the Canadian Northern and the American-owned Rutland Railroad — both of whom saw the CAR as a natural extension of their own systems.

The CAR consisted of two merged, Booth-built railways: the original Canada Atlantic Railway, running between Ottawa, Ontario, Côteau, Quebec and East Alburgh, Vermont and the Ottawa–Madawaska–Depot Harbour, Ontario, Ottawa Arnprior & Parry Sound Railway. Shortly after the 1883 opening of the CAR between Côteau and Ottawa, Booth's railroad was drawn into the Grank Trunk camp. His through passenger trains began operating between Ottawa and Montreal in conjunction with the GTR. The CAR/GTR passenger trains were in hot competition with the CPR and boasted the first electrically illuminated equipment in Canada. By the turn of the century, the high-speed CAR–GTR/CPR rivalry spawned a trio of CAR Baldwin-built, Vauclain compound 4–4–2s, including No. 618, whose 84½-inch drivers remain the largest of any Canadian locomotive in history. After its sale to the Grand Trunk, the original CAR Côteau–Ottawa line became the key link in GTR's Montreal–Ottawa mainline — a role it continues to serve today.

When built by Booth during the 1890s, the 263.8-mile Ottawa–Depot Harbour OA&PS was divided into two operating divisions. Madawaska, nearly midway between Ottawa and Depot Harbour, was established as the division point, and was provided with an expansive yard, roundhouse and shop facilities. The OA&PS thrived on lumber traffic (and connected with several logging branches), as well as overhead tonnage between CAR's Vermont connections and Depot Harbour. In the harbour Booth's steamships of the Canada Atlantic Transit Co. handled coal, grain and merchandise to and from Midwestern Great Lakes ports. Six-coupled power — Moguls, Ten-Wheelers and a very rare, standard-gauge "Mason–Fairlie Bogie" (CAR 0–6–6 No. 8) — dominated the CAR roster, but 14 brawny, Baldwin-built Vauclain Compound 2–8–0s were the backbone of the OA&PS freight power.

Although purchased by the Grand Trunk in 1905, the Canada Atlantic retained its identity until merged into the Grand Trunk system in 1913. By this time, the mighty Grand Trunk Railway was headed for a fall.

THE INTERCOLONIAL RAILWAY

The selection of Portland, Maine, rather than Halifax, Nova Scotia, as the ocean terminal of the Grand Trunk deflated maritime Canada's long-nurtured dream of a mainline link with the rest of the country. Alienated from the west, the Maritime provinces embarked on an independent course of railway development but never lost sight of their dreams of a mainline. When the British North America Act of July 1, 1867 united the provinces of Ontario, Quebec, Nova Scotia and New Brunswick as the Dominion of Canada, one of the key

promises of confederation was a mainline railway linking the Maritime provinces with the rest of the Dominion. Clause 145 fulfilled the agreement, promising prompt construction of the Intercolonial Railway of Canada (IRC).

At the time of confederation, Nova Scotia and New Brunswick had but three significant shortlines, with a total of only 288 miles. The disorganized maritime network was made up of: the grand-sounding European & North American Railway, opened in August 1860, between Saint John, New Brunswick (on the Bay of Fundy) and Shediac, N.B. on the Northumberland Strait; the New Brunswick & Canada Railway, running from St. Andrew's, N.B., to Woodstock, N.B. with a branch from St. Stephen to Watt Junction; and the 145-mile Nova Scotia Railway, built between Halifax, Truro and Pictou, Nova Scotia with a 32-mile branch from the mainline just beyond Halifax to Windsor, Nova Scotia, on the Bay of Fundy. The Nova Scotia Railway is credited with one of the earliest piggyback operations — carrying farmers' wagons (their horses loaded into separate boxcars) and even carrying stagecoaches on trains in and out of Halifax. At one point, the piggyback business was responsible for one-quarter of the total freight revenue of the Nova Scotia Railway.

While the New Brunswick & Canada Railway was destined to become part of the CPR, the European & North American and the Nova Scotia Railway were incorporated into the Intercolonial Railway being built between Halifax and the Grand Trunk connection at Rivière du Loup, Quebec.

In spite of patronage, corruption and other scandals plaguing it, the Intercolonial, by virtue of the intelligence and devotion of its engineer-in-chief Sanford Fleming, was well built. At Fleming's insistence, the IRC con-

structed iron, rather than wooden bridges, laid superior-quality steel rails and converted to standard gauge while still under construction.

The Intercolonial was completed in June 1876, and in July a through train from Halifax to Quebec officially marked completion of the railroad uniting the provinces. Observers extolled the virtues of the new railway and exclaimed that its value to the nation could not be measured in dollars. There were those, primarily in political office, who quickly placed a dollar value on the line and opened a season of corruption, patronage and greed that would eclipse that of the building years. Supply contracts were handed out to political cronies; special trains were operated — free of charge — for senators, members of parliament and members of legislative assemblies. Trains were provided at a flat rate of $10 (regardless of distance) for political rallies and elections. Discipline was also a problem encountered during the early years of operation; crews stopped trains on a whim, coal from locomotive tenders found its way to home stoves, and

The occasion prompting a portrait photo of Intercolonial Railway No. 66 is unknown, but the 4-4-0 and company are suitably polished for the event. *Public Archives Canada*

An example of the high-grade construction employed on the Intercolonial, ICR 4–6–0 No. 69 poses on an embankment in the Wentworth Valley in Nova Scotia, sometime in the early 1900s. *Public Archives Canada*

drunkenness went undisciplined. It would take early managers more than a decade to bring the system to heel. And despite its beginning, the Intercolonial became a responsible operation building an impressive, if not profitable, maritime system. The company took bankrupt shortlines under its wing and soon stretched from the southern tip of Nova Scotia to Sydney, on Cape Breton Island, blanketed New Brunswick and, by virtue of trackage rights over the Grand Trunk, extended west to Montreal.

THE PRINCE EDWARD ISLAND RAILWAY

Prince Edward Island, for its own reasons, avoided joining the Dominion of Canada until 1873. As a condition of entry at that time, the Island government insisted that its partially completed and already troubled Prince Edward Island Railway be taken over and operated by the dominion. After considerable negotiation, the federal government inherited a narrow-gauge (3′6″) railroad. The Island Government paid contractors by the mile. Thus the Railway's trackage wandered almost aimlessly about the island as it ran from tip to tip, originating at Tignish in the west and terminating at Souris in the east, with branches to the capital at Charlottetown and to Georgetown, midway down the eastern coast.

In the tradition of so many early Canadian lines, the PEIR ordered its original locomotives from England . . . and in the continuing tradition of many early Canadian railroads, the PEIR quickly discovered that the English engines (in this case six 4–4–0Ts built by Hanslet Engine Company of Leeds, England) were too light and generally unsuitable for Canadian duty. The British engines were replaced with a fleet of Baldwins and Canadian Locomotive Company 4–4–0s that were the line's staple power until the purchase of heavier 4–6–0s that began arriving from CLC's Kingston works in 1907.

Despite the island's small size and its railroad's large operating deficits, several branchlines were built during the late 1800s and early 1900s. In 1885, a line was opened between Emerald Junction and Cape Traverse to connect with ferry service to the mainland. Further expansion was limited to the east side of the island, with branches to Murray Harbour, Vernon and Montague completed in 1905–1906 and a line to Elmira in 1912. Islanders were oblivious to the fact that their tiny railroad lost more money in some years than the entire Intercolonial Railroad — an outfit five times larger than the PEIR.

World War I interrupted a government programme to upgrade PEI's link with the mainland, but by 1917, the Cape Traverse line had been re-routed to the new car ferry terminal at Borden. In 1918, ferry service between Borden, PEI and Cape Tormentine, New Brunswick, was bolstered by the addition of the 12-car–capacity ice-breaking car ferry *Prince Edward Island.*

With reliable, year-round car-ferry service established, the government turned its attention to standard-gauging the 277-mile PEIR. At the close of World War I, rails rolled in U.S. steel mills for supply to Russia were diverted to PEI and the lines between Borden, Summerside and Charlottetown were dual-gauged. Title to the PEIR was transferred to the newly formed Canadian National Railways in 1918 and by 1923 orders were issued to standard-gauge the entire island railroad. Conversion of the west end, from Tignish to Royalty Junction, was accomplished in the first year, but work on the east end was delayed. The lines to Elmira, Souris, Georgetown and Montague were standard-gauged in 1926, but the 42–inch gauge remained in use on the Murray Harbour/ Vernon branch until 1930. The narrow-gauge era on Prince Edward Island finally came to a close on September 27, 1930, when high-headlighted CN 4–6–0 No. 34 (a CLC graduate of 1918) brought the local from Murray Harbour and Vernon into Charlottetown.

Former Intercolonial Railway 4–4–0 No. 150, purchased secondhand for use in construction on the north shore of Lake Superior, poses on a temporary, 80-foot-high, 600-foot-long timber trestle over the Pic River. *Canadian Pacific*

am neither a prophet, nor the son of a prophet, yet . . . I believe that many in this room will live to hear the whistle of the steam engine in the passes of the Rocky Mountains and to make the journey from Halifax to the Pacific in five or six days." — Joseph Howe, Halifax, May 15, 1851.

Sir John A. Macdonald, the first Canadian prime minister, came to share Joseph Howe's dream and was intent upon seeing it brought to fruition. In an attempt to woo British Columbia into confederation, Macdonald promised to build a railway to the Pacific. The west coast province accepted and on July 20, 1871, British Columbia joined the Dominion of Canada — with the Pacific railway as a precondition.

Article II of the Order-in-Council Respecting the Province of British Columbia committed the government of Canada to make good the promise. "The Government of the Dominion undertakes to secure the commencement simultaneously, within two years from the date of union, of the construction of a railway from the Pacific towards the Rocky Mountains, and from such point as may be selected east of the Rocky Mountains towards the Pacific, to connect the seaboard of British Columbia with the railway system of Canada; and further, to secure the completion of such railway within ten years from the date of union . . ."

With those 78 words, Article II would set in motion a series of events that would: topple the Macdonald government in the Pacific Scandal of 1873; see British Columbia threaten to secede from confederation as a protest to Macdonald's successor's inaction on the Pacific railway; restore Macdonald to power in 1878 and ultimately result, albeit somewhat later than the promised ten years, in the completion of an iron road from sea to sea. At Craigellachie, British Columbia, in the early morning cool of November 7, 1885, Donald A. Smith drove home the last spike of the Canadian Pacific Railway. Canada was now united both in spirit and in deed. Macdonald's promise to B.C. was made good, and as steam whistles echoed through the Rocky Mountain passes, the prophecy of Joseph Howe was fulfilled.

THE PEMBINA BRANCH

Originally undertaken as a government project, operation of the Canadian Pacific Railway began, not with the legendary east–west mainline, but with the Pembina branch — a 63-mile line between St. Boniface, Manitoba (opposite Winnipeg) and the U.S. border at Emerson, where it connected with the St. Paul & Pacific Railway (later the St. Paul Minneapolis & Manitoba Railway).

On October 9, 1877, the sternwheeler *Selkirk* chugged down the Red River to Winnipeg/St. Boniface, shoving a barge bearing six flatcars, a conductors' van and an ex-Northern Pacific 4–4–0, which was the first locomotive to reach the Canadian prairies. Lettered Canadian Pacific No. 1, the engine was christened *Countess of Dufferin* in honour of the wife of the visiting Canadian governor general, the Earl of

Soon to be christened the *Countess of Dufferin*, Joseph Whitehead's ex-Northern Pacific 4–4–0, lettered "Canadian Pacific No. 1" arrives at Winnipeg, Manitoba, October 9, 1877, on a barge pushed by the sternwheeler *Selkirk*. *Canadian Pacific*

Dufferin. The hand-me-down Baldwin eight-wheeler was the property of Pembina branch contractor Joseph Whitehead, as were the similarly-lettered seven cars. After an appropriate ceremony the equipment was unloaded at St. Boniface and pressed into work-train service, supplying construction and track-laying crews on the Pembina branch and later on the mainline east of Winnipeg. The *Countess* is still extant in Winnipeg, first put on display in 1910 by a city very conscious of its railway heritage.

Whitehead purchased a second 4–4–0 during 1878 and on December 5 of that year, the Pembina branch saw its first train. The federal government took over the line on February 10, 1880, and initiated daily service between St. Boniface and the Minnesota border, while a twice-weekly train ran north to Selkirk and east on the mainline as far as Cross Lake.

FORGING AHEAD

Construction on the Pacific railway proper got underway on June 1, 1875, with the turning of the first sod at the lakehead location of what is now Thunder Bay. For over seven years, railway construction crews working west from Thunder Bay and east from the banks of the Red River at Selkirk pushed the railroad through forbidding territory. Bottomless muskegs swallowed completed roadbed and track under the weight of work trains; passage was inhibited by rocky terrain and countless lakes; and the merciless cold of winter was only relieved by the blistering heat and voracious black flies of summer.

As work on the Thunder Bay section progressed, there was action on all fronts. Sir John A. Macdonald recovered from the Pacific Scandal of 1873 (the result of his efforts to find private financing for the Pacific railway) and was re-elected to the office of prime minister in 1878. Under Macdonald, the Pacific railway forged ahead with renewed vigour. The Red River was bridged at Winnipeg and construction moved west across Manitoba prairie. On the Pacific coast separatist notions were dispelled as New York contractor Andrew Onderdonk began building the railroad through the Fraser River Canyon on May 14, 1880. Back in the east, the House of Commons passed an act incorporating the Canadian Pacific Railway Company on February 15, 1881.

EXTENDING THE CPR

Heir to the transcontinental railway, the CPR immediately set about extending itself beyond the government-intended terminus at Callander and into the heart of populated

eastern Canada. In order to connect the Pacific railway with the rest of the Canadian railway system, the government had been financing extension of the Canada Central Railway from its former terminus at Sand Point to the CPR railhead at Callander. Canadian Pacific quickly acquired this line and on June 9, 1881, the

Canada Central became part of the CPR.

Although it would be years before the mainline across northern Ontario would link east and west, the CPR had established its presence in eastern Canada. The 254-mile Canada Central gave the CPR a line from Brockville to Mattawa (and still pushing west

toward Callander) as well as branch lines from Carleton Place to Ottawa and from Smith Falls to Perth. The CCR, a former broad-gauge road dating back to the 1853 chartering of the Brockville & Ottawa, forms a significant part of CPR's current eastern Ontario network. The B&O is historically significant also because of its tunnel underneath the town of Brockville. Built by 1860, it is Canada's oldest.

Onderdonk's army of more than 7,000 men blasted, bridged and tunnelled their way through the Fraser River canyon, track-laying crews pushed west across the prairie and crews on the Thunder Bay section closed in on the meeting point west of Eagle River, while CPR offices in the east concentrated on building up a regional network to complement the transcontinental mainline.

CPR vs. GTR

The Canada Central deal was sewn up and construction progressed toward Callander. The CPR was now set to gain access to Montreal, site of the company's headquarters and the largest city in Canada at the time. Running between Ottawa, at the end of one of the former Canada Central branches, and Montreal, with branches to Aylmer, Quebec and St. Jerome, Quebec, the western division of the Quebec, Montreal, Ottawa and Occidental Railway fit the bill perfectly and was purchased in the spring of 1882. At the same time, two shortlines connecting with the QMO&O at Ste. Therese and St. Lin Junction were acquired. Trackage rights over the North Shore Railway (eastern division of QMO&O) between St. Martin Junction and Quebec City were secured at the time of the western division purchase, setting the stage for one of the earliest conflicts between the CPR and the Grand Trunk.

Canadian Pacific's eastern expansion was encroaching upon the near monopoly the Grand Trunk enjoyed in the region. To protect its threatened territory, the GTR executed a series of defensive moves, including purchase of the North Shore Railway in 1883. Under the impression that the North Shore's QMO&O trackage rights into Montreal had been part of the package, the GTR constructed the Jacques Cartier Union Railway to link the two properties. The CPR was silent on the matter until the branch was complete; then the company withdrew the GTR rights. Grand Trunk responded with cancellation of CPR's running rights over the North Shore to Quebec City. The federal government was drawn into the fray and as the air cleared, the North Shore was the property of the Canadian Pacific Railway.

Continuing to spread its tentacles throughout the east, the CPR acquired the South Eastern

Top: Employed by Andrew Onderdonk and Co. on construction of the Pacific Section, the *Nicola* sports an improvised tender after losing her original in one of many derailments. *Canadian Pacific*

Bottom: The predecessor to the familiar caboose or "van" was little more than a modified boxcar. *Ontario Archives*

Railway in Quebec. The company also resuscitated the charter of the still-born Ontario & Quebec Railway in 1881 as a means of building a Toronto–Montreal mainline. The new line incorporated the recently annexed QMO&O from Montreal to Ottawa, the former Canada Central from Ottawa, through Smith Falls to Perth and construction of the O&Q from Perth through Peterborough to Toronto.

Before the O&Q was even complete, the CPR swallowed a series of southwestern Ontario shortlines that would firmly entrench the Canadian Pacific in the Grand Trunk's richest traffic stronghold. On January 4, 1884, Canadian Pacific leased the Ontario & Quebec Railway Company for 999 years along with the 184.1-mile Perth–West Toronto line. The lease included the following O&Q acquisitions:

- The Credit Valley Railway, with a 122-mile Toronto–St. Thomas mainline, as well as branches from Streetsville to Elora and Orangeville.
- The London Junction Railway, a CVR leasehold with a charter to build from the CVR mainline at Woodstock to London, 27 miles west.
- The Toronto Grey and Bruce Railway, a former narrow-gauge line, built from Toronto to the Georgian Bay port of Owen Sound, with a 68-mile branch from Fraxa (just north of Orangeville) to Mount Forest and Teeswater.

Although most of O&Q itself would be downgraded to secondary status with the opening of the Toronto–Perth Lakeshore Line in 1914, all three of its acquisitions would be of great significance in the immediate and/or long-term future of the Canadian Pacific Railway. The Credit Valley gave CP a route west of Toronto and an invaluable connection with the Michigan Central (Canada Southern) at St. Thomas. To this day the former CVR/London Jct. route forms half of CP's Toronto–Windsor mainline.

Acquisition of the Toronto Grey & Bruce would reshape the intended rail-water route between Montreal and Port Arthur. The TG&B's Georgian Bay outlet at Owen Sound was of superior quality and 100 miles closer to Montreal than the planned port at Algoma Mills on the north channel of Lake Huron. Within days of the TG&B takeover, construction on the Algoma branch, linking Algoma Mills with the mainline near Sudbury, was suspended and plans for extensive port and rail facilities at Algoma Mills were shelved. While Algoma Mills was never revived, the Algoma branch remained in limbo until 1888, when it was extended west to Sault Ste. Marie.

In May 1884, Canadian Pacific inaugurated steamship service between Owen Sound and Port Arthur. The last spike on the mainline between the Lakehead and Winnipeg had been

driven on June 19, 1882, but regular trains had been operating for less than a year. For the Western Division, 1884 would mark the first full year of operation. The newly-opened line would be taxed to the limit with the completion of grain elevators at Port Arthur and Fort William, the establishment of steamship service to the east, and the heavy westbound flow of construction materials bound for supply crews pushing the railroad across the prairie and into the mountains.

(The names of towns can get confusing here. Fort William and the twin town of Port Arthur grew together and were commonly known as the Lakehead. In 1976 the two towns amalgamated into a new municipality known as Thunder Bay.)

West of the Lakehead, forests echoed with the exhaust of polished, cap-stacked 4–4–0s wheeling passengers to Winnipeg; trackage laid over bottomless muskeg wowed under the weight of grain trains rumbling eastward; and

track laid before the end of 1882. During 1882, the mainline advanced westward by 418 miles — stopping just short of Maple Creek, 585 miles west of Winnipeg, in January 1883. The southwestern branch added 110 miles of new trackage in Manitoba, for a total of 528 miles of mainline — plus an additional 57 miles of sidings constructed. Settlers followed in the wake of the roadroad and the CPR literally opened up the Canadian west.

Throughout 1883, the railroad pushed westward, often at a record-breaking pace. Track-laying crews regularly racked up impressive tallies of over four miles per day and set a system-wide record of 6.38 miles spiked down on June 28. Medicine Hat, Alberta, was east of the railhead by June; the first train reached Calgary in August; and at the end of the track-laying season in November 1883, the railhead was little more than a mile short of the Continental Divide.

If 1883 was to be remembered as a year of record-breaking progress across the prairies, then 1884 should be recorded as a year of spectacular effort and expense poured into carving a railroad out of some of the most hostile terrain on the continent. Crews, fresh from the drive across the prairies, headed up the Bow River into the Rockies toward Kicking Horse Pass. Onderdonk's forces continued to push east through the mountains. Simultaneously, railway builders east of the Lakehead fought sinkholes, unstable rock formations and violent storms in their efforts to notch a railroad into the rocky north shore of Lake Superior. To expedite completion of the line north of Superior, men, materials and equipment — including locomotives and rolling stock — were sailed into several remote locations along the north shore. Crews labouring year round out of Mazokama, McKay's Harbour, Jackfish Bay and Heron Bay were hampered by bad weather and the interruption of lake-borne supply lines. The men built towering trestles and massive rock fills, bored tunnels and blasted hundreds of rock cuts to push the CPR through country as treacherous as it was spectacular. Gradually, the gaps were filled, trestles and tunnels completed and sinkholes — after consuming hundreds of cars of fill — were stabilized. The last spike on the Montreal–Winnipeg mainline of the CPR was driven near Jackfish Bay in mid-May, 1885. Several more months were spent completing trackwork and ballasting, establishing division points (approximately 125 miles apart) and constructing stations, sidings, water towers and other support facilities. Montreal–Winnipeg freight service began in October and the first week of November saw inauguration of through passenger trains.

Construction of the entire CPR east of the Rocky Mountain foothills pales in comparison to the unequalled achievement of scratching

The Columbia River bridge near Revelstoke, B.C. supports a work train, powered by nearly-new CPR No. 365, a 4-4-0 outshopped by the Canadian Locomotive Co. in 1886. *Public Archives Canada*

a winter's worth of locomotive coal moved west at the rate of two fifteen-car trains a day. Between trains, track crews fought to keep the muskeg from swallowing the mainline (piles had to be driven 135 feet deep to stabilize the line near Oxdrift). They replaced miles of worn-out or faulty rail, rebuilt bridges to support the increased tonnage and somehow found the time to carry out ongoing maintenance of the rest of the line.

PUSHING WESTWARD

Under the direction of William Cornelius Van Horne — probably the most famous and most respected name in Canadian railroad history — the CPR was pushed across the prairies with impressive speed and efficiency. As general manager, Van Horne took the reigns on December 31, 1881, and shortly thereafter announced that he would have 500 miles of

the single-track CP mainline through the successive mountain ranges from the Pacific coast at Port Moody to the eastern edge of Kicking Horse Pass. An account of the lives and labour, the tons of rock, forests of lumber, millions of ties and the miles of steel spent in laying just 554 miles of railroad could fill volumes. More than five and a half years passed between the detonation of the first explosion at Yale, B.C. and the driving of the last spike at Craigellachie.

ON TO THE PACIFIC

Andrew Onderdonk, under government and later Canadian Pacific contracts, got construction of the Pacific section underway on May 14, 1880. Responsible for the stretch between Port Moody and Eagle Pass, Onderdonk's largely Chinese forces built a railroad that poked in and out of tunnels, rode miles of spindly trestlework and taunted raging Fraser waters. A fleet of steam locomotives, ranging from hand-me-down engines from Virginia & Truckee in Nevada to newly-bought Baldwin 4–4–0 powered work trains, ran the supplies on land while the sternwheeler *Skuzzy* winched up the "unnavigable" Fraser and Thompson rivers, transporting supplies to work gangs beyond the railhead. The railroad advanced eastward through the mountains at a cost of millions of dollars and countless lives — many lost in rock slides, tunnel collapses, and numerous, often spectacular derailments. By January 1884, trains were transporting girders 136 miles inland to the site of the canti-lever bridge being erected across the Fraser River at Cisco. With the arrival of summer the

$269,000 bridge was complete and by the fall of 1884 trains were operating as far east as Spences Bridge. Onderdonk's men reached Eagle Pass and completed their work by early October 1885, a month before the arrival of crews from the east.

THE BIG HILL

On the eastern front, CPR crews under the direction of James Ross crossed the Continental Divide on May 25, 1884 and ran head-on into a problem. Surveys indicated that to maintain gradients below the established maximum of 2.2 percent, the line would have to cross many known avalanche paths, tunnel 1,400 feet through Mount Stephen and make a 15 mile, 2.2 percent descent to the banks of Kicking Horse River. The alternative was a 4.5 mile, 4.5 percent grade between Wapta Lake and the base of Mount Stephen. In the name of both expediency and lower construction costs, the latter option was chosen and the legendary "Big Hill" was born. As protection against the inevitable runaways, three safety tracks were constructed on the "Hill." With switch points facing down-bound trains, these dead-end sidings diverged from the mainline and angled steeply upgrade. Switches were kept lined for the safety tracks so that if runaways occurred (and they did) the uncontrolled trains would exit the mainline and be slowed by the upgrade siding. Switch tenders manned the safety tracks and after down-bound trains made the mandatory stop at each point, lined the switch for the mainline. After the passage of each train, switches would be relined to the

A massive brute compared to contemporary 4–4–0's, CPR No. 315 is one of several Baldwin 2–8–0's specially built to conquer the 4.5 percent grades of the Big Hill east of Field, B.C. *Public Archives Canada*

Working its intended territory, CPR No. 315 pauses at one of the safety tracks (visible on the left) on the Big Hill. *Canadian Pacific*

"normal" diverging route.

The Big Hill was intended to serve only as a temporary solution to the problem of putting the railroad over Kicking Horse Pass. The permanent route would be decided only after studies of climatic conditions and avalanche patterns were completed. In this instance temporary translated to a quarter of a century of pitting men and machines against the greatest operating challenge of the entire CPR. As difficult as it was to boost tonnage up the gruelling 4.5 percent, the task of easing trains down the treacherous grade was more challenging — indeed, hazardous. The constant threat of runaways hung over the heads of "Hill crews" and until completion of the spiral tunnels closed the Big Hill in 1909, the safety tracks earned their keep.

Putting the Big Hill behind them, Ross's construction gangs pushed west. On the eastern slope of the Selkirks, they used over two million board feet of timber in construction of the 164-foot high, 1,086-foot long Mountain Creek Bridge. They crossed Stoney Creek on one of the highest bridges in the world and descended the west slope of the Selkirks using a series of loops — the most impressive are at Illecilliwaet that kept gradients within the desired 2.2 percent maximum. The work was plagued by strikes and avalanches, forest fires and floods, and nearly bankrupted the CPR. In spite of it all, only three and a half miles separated the east and west railheads by November 5, 1885.

With engines working front and rear, a Canadian Pacific passenger train stands on the 292-foot-high Stoney Creek Trestle. *Public Archives Canada*

Bottom: Canadian Pacific S.D. class 2–8–0 No. 403, built at the company's "New Shops" in Montreal in 1886, is spotted for the photographer on the Mountain Creek bridge. Containing more than two million board-feet of lumber, the 1,086-foot-long, 164-foot high bridge was the largest on the CPR at the time. *Canadian Pacific Collection*

MEETING AT CRAIGELLACHIE

Long before the railroad was completed, Van Horne had declared that the site of the last spike, wherever it may be, would be named Craigellachie — in honour of the invaluable services of George Stephen, the CPR's first president, and CPR director Donald Smith (Stephen's cousin and later Lord Strathcona) — whose ancestors had once rallied in the Spey Valley of Scotland at a crag known as Craigellachie. Van Horne further ruled that there would be no golden spike and no great ceremony for driving the last spike.

Using a primitive electric generator and lights, Ross's men laid track night and day to close the gap. Van Horne, Donald Smith, John Egan, Sanford Fleming and a small group of family and friends arrived on a special train from Montreal as the last rails were being cut to size. With little fanfare, the group assembled and at 09:22 Pacific time, east met west at Craigellachie as Donald Smith drove home a plain iron spike joining rails that spanned the nation.

Van Horne closed the brief ceremony with a simple speech limited to fifteen words: "All I can say is that the work has been well done in every way."

Van Horne's party continued west to Port Moody and their train, led by 4–4–0 No. 148, became the first to cross Canada. The route through the mountains was far from complete — stations, sidings, snowsheds and support and maintenance facilities had still to be built. As a symbolic gesture, the CPR accepted a transcontinental shipment of 40 drums of oil billed from the Halifax Naval Dockyard to the dockyard at Esquimalt, B.C. But after passage of the Naval Supply Extra and the eastbound return of Van Horne's train, the mountain section of the mainline was shut down until spring.

Throughout the winter, engineers based at mountain camps along the line observed and recorded avalanche and weather patterns to determine the locations of snow sheds.

Snowplows and manpower dug out the line in the spring and construction resumed. Miles of snowsheds were built to protect the line from avalanches, track was ballasted, cuts widened and support facilities constructed.

On Monday, June 28, 1886, CPR train No. 1, the "Pacific Express," left Montreal for the west coast. One hundred and thirty-nine hours and 2,892.6 miles later, 4–4–0 No. 371 eased the train into the CPR station at Port Moody, British Columbia. Transcontinental service was a reality.

Completion of the transcontinental mainline was but a beginning for the CPR. A 12.5-mile extension from Port Moody to Vancouver was underway even before cross-country service was inaugurated, and while the country marvelled at the new railroad to the Pacific, the CPR was aggressively pursuing expansion in the east, notably toward the Atlantic.

At 8:30 P.M. on June 2, 1889 — less than three years after the inaugural run of the "Pacific Express," the first CPR train to the east coast pulled out of the Windsor Station in Montreal. The four-car train, led by CP 4–4–0 No. 147 (ex-TG&B 25) as far as Megantic, was the first through train over the Short Line, a 481-mile short cut between Montreal and St. John, New Brunswick.

More than 200 miles shorter than the all-Canada GTR/IRC route to St. John, the Short Line cut across southern Quebec, northern Maine and into New Brunswick over a route that comprised a new line built between Montreal and Sherbrooke (including a bridge built over the St. Lawrence River at Lachine); the former International Railway between Sherbrooke and Megantic, acquired in 1887; a new line constructed from Megantic through

One of 24 locomotives used on the first scheduled transcontinental passenger train, CPR No. 33, a Scottish-built 4–4–0, heads the first run of the Montreal–Port Moody "Pacific Express" at Fort William, Ont. on June 30, 1886. *Canadian Pacific Collection*

Canadian Pacific 4–4–0 No. 374 is appropriately decorated for participation in ceremonies celebrating completion of the CPR line into Port Moody, B.C. *Public Archives Canada*

Bottom: Five years before the railway was leased to the CPR, a New Brunswick Railway 4–4–0 hauls a train of new boxcars over the cantilever bridge over the famed Reversing Falls of the St. John River at St. John, N.B. *Canadian Pacific Collection*

the backwoods of Maine to a junction with the Maine Central at Mattawamkeag, Maine; trackage rights over the MEC to Vanceboro, Maine on the New Brunswick border and passage over the New Brunswick Railway into St. John.

On September 1, 1890, the CPR acquired the New Brunswick Railway, giving the company title to the Vanceboro, Me.–St. John, N.B. mainline, as well as branches to Edmunston, Fredericton, St. Stephen and St. Andrews, New Brunswick. Including the 56-mile trackage rights over the Maine Central, the Canadian Pacific Railway had established itself as the first true transcontinental railroad in North America. Its status as such would go unchallenged for more than a quarter century.

EXPANSION OF THE CPR

With Van Horne elevated to the presidency in 1889 and a mainline that spanned the dominion from sea to sea, the CPR embarked on an ambitious programme of expansion and capital improvement that would carry on well into the 20th century. Feeder lines and branchlines sprouted from the mainline, criss-crossing the eastern provinces and blanketing the prairies.

The Montreal–Toronto mainline was dramatically shortened with the construction of a new line between Montreal and Smith Falls, Ontario. In southern Ontario, the former Credit Valley line was extended from Woodstock through London to Windsor — tapping the motherlode of lucrative U.S. transit traffic.

Meanwhile, in British Columbia, steam-powered CPR sternwheelers were plying the inland lakes, Upper Arrow and Lower Arrow and Kootenay. A branch from the mainline at Revelstoke to the slips on Upper Arrow Lake at Arrowhead linked the lake services with the outside world. To the south, an isolated CPR branchline, built in 1891 as the Columbia and Kootenay, portaged an unnavigable section of the Kootenay River between Robson and Nelson, forming a land bridge between Kootenay Lake and the Arrow Lakes.

The CPR was not alone in the Kootenays though. Mineral wealth and growing resource traffic had attracted American interests and a battle was brewing over who would dominate the region.

COMPETITION IN THE KOOTENAYS

Van Horne cringed when Daniel Corbin's Spokane Falls & Northern, known as the Nelson & Fort Sheppard north of the border, pushed into southern B.C., reaching Five-Mile Point, five miles east of Nelson on the south shore of the western leg of Kootenay Lake, in 1893. With his own line to Nelson, Van Horne could handle the competition. But in 1895, when arch-rival James J. Hill's Great Northern financed construction of the isolated three-foot–gauge Kaslo and Slocan, the war was on.

In direct competition with the CPR, Hill had already brought the GN up the west coast to New Westminster, B.C. To have Great Northern in the Kootenays as well was more than Van Horne could tolerate. With assistance from the federal and provincial governments, the CPR countered the GN intrusion with construction of the Nakusp & Slocan.

Nestled high in the Slocan range between Slocan and Kootenay lakes, Sandon, British Columbia, site of rich deposits of silver and lead, was the common destination of both roads. While the K&S struck out from Kaslo on the west side of Kootenay Lake, the CPR's Nakusp & Slocan built eastward from Nakusp on the shores of Upper Arrow Lake. Hill's railroad reached Sandon in October, well ahead of its Canadian rival. To show the flag, the CPR responded with construction of an imposing station and freight shed in Sandon — weeks before its own rails reached town. The ball was in Hill's court, and the tone of bitter confrontations to come was set in the pre-dawn darkness of December 16, 1895. A trainload of

A short train on Daniel Corbin's Nelson & Fort Sheppard meets the sternwheeler *S.S. Nelson* at Five Mile Point, B.C.
Provincial Archives of British Columbia

Kaslo & Slocan men rolled into Sandon, destroying a CPR trestle as well as the new freight shed — and in the ultimate gesture of contempt, strung a cable from the station to a waiting locomotive . . . a tug on the throttle brought the CPR's handsome station crashing down. The GN/CP feud carried on, province-wide, for years. The repercussions of the clash in the Kootenays would affect railroading on a nationwide scale.

At the height of the conflict, both GN and CP operations in the Kootenays were isolated from their respective mainlines. Their sole connections to the outside world were the stern-wheelers, tugs and car barges sailing the inland lakes. In view of the vast mineral wealth of the Kootenays — which included significant deposits of copper, lead, silver, zinc and coal — both railroads were totally inadequate.

For Hill, the region's proximity to the U.S. border — and the GN mainline — made the solution simple. In a multi-pronged attack, GN bought Corbin's SF&N/N&FS in 1898 and in succeeding years built several other branch-lines into the southern reaches of B.C.

Canadian Pacific was confronted with a more significant challenge. The only practical way to gain access to the Kootenays was to build another east–west line into British Columbia. The cost of a second line through the mountains

would be staggering, but the company — and indeed, the country — could not allow the tremendous mineral wealth of the Kootenays to flow exclusively south of the border. Citing the national interest in having a Canadian railroad serving southern British Columbia, Van Horne sought government aid for construction of a line from Fort McLeod, Northwest Territories (now Alberta), through Crows Nest Pass and west to Kootenay Landing, British Columbia.

The British Columbia government responded with a land grant totalling 3,755,733 acres (50,000 coal-bearing acres included in the grant were later transferred to the federal government). In June, 1897, the infamous Crows Nest Pass Agreement guaranteed the southern B.C. line a federal subsidy of $11,000 per mile in exchange for certain concessions from the CPR. The federal monies would total more than 3.4 million dollars and cover approximately one-third of the construction costs. "The Crow," as the legislation would come to be known, would haunt the CPR — and subsequently all grain-handling Canadian railroads — for 88 years.

Among the concessions agreed to was a reduction and freeze on freight rates charged for movement of selected commodities, including grain. Amendments to the agreement eventually removed all rate restrictions —

Working CP's isolated Vancouver Island subsidiary, the Esquimalt & Nanaimo, CPR Ten-Wheeler No. 229 eases a four-car wooden passenger consist to a stop at the waterfront depot at Cameron Lake, B.C. *Canadian Pacific Collection*

except those on grain — which instead, were expanded to include all Canadian railroads. Until 1984 (with only a brief break during World War I) Canadian railroads paid the price of extending the CPR into the Kootenays, as "The Crow" kept grain rates pegged at turn-of-the-century levels.

Van Horne wasted little time getting the line built. By the fall of 1898, CPR trains were marching their way to the 4,579-foot summit of Crows Nest Pass, en route to Kootenay Landing. Due to the difficulties of building along Kootenay Lake, traffic was ferried over the lake from Kootenay Landing to Procter, where trackage resumed. Construction continued west, connecting with the previously isolated line between Nelson and Robson, but British Columbians' dreams of a second mainline across the province died when the line halted at Midway, early in 1900.

Mining, smelting and lumbering operations in the Kootenays boomed with the railroad's arrival. And although the Great Northern maintained a strong presence, the CPR also prospered with the region. Van Horne's share of the Kootenay wealth was enhanced with the acquisition of the Columbia & Western Railway between Robson and Trail, along with a smelter at Trail that formed the foundation of CP's Consolidated Mining & Smelting Co. Cominco subsidiary.

THE KETTLE VALLEY RAILWAY

Great Northern threats to build east from Vancouver to the Kootenays prompted the CPR to revive plans to complete the line across southern B.C. Opened in 1916, between Midway and the junction with the mainline at Petain (now Odlum), CP's Kettle Valley Railway was mountain railroading at its toughest. Tangent track was a rarity; heavy grades — including Canada's longest sustained 2.2 percent between Penticton and Chute Lake — were the rule; tunnels (including a 1,604-foot spiral near Carmir, B.C.), bridges and snowsheds often averaged better than one per mile. Slides and washouts were a constant threat — particularly west of Brodie, where an angered Coquihalla Pass was forever trying to shake the railroad from its shoulders.

Although technically a through route, the southern mainline was still hampered by the gap between Kootenay Landing and Procter. Barge services bridged the break until completion of a line hugging the shore of Kootenay Lake was completed between the two points in 1931.

The expansion that characterized the turn of the century continued through the early 1900s. Significant acquisitions were made in 1912, with the leasing of the Esquimalt & Nanaimo Railway (on Vancouver Island), the Quebec

In the Upper Canyon of the Kicking Horse River, three engines, led by 4–6–0 No. 562, power an eight-car, eastbound CPR Passenger train on the 4.5 percent Big Hill, about 1910. *Canadian Pacific Collection*

Right: The westbound "Pacific Express" rolls over the new steel Stoney Creek trestle, built in 1893 to replace the original wooden bridge. *Canadian Pacific Collection*

Central Railway and Nova Scotia's Dominion Atlantic Railway. However, the period was highlighted by extensive rebuilding of the original mainline through the mountains of British Columbia.

TUNNELLING THROUGH

In 1902, the Ottertail Diversion relocated several miles of mainline between Field and Ottertail and eliminated the need for helper service over the Muskeg Summit west of Field. East of Field, the Big Hill remained an operating nightmare. The ever-real threat of runaways severely restricted the size of down-bound trains and in spite of larger road power and compound 2–8–0 pushers, upgrade tonnage restrictions were equally limited. Even passenger trains required three or more engines (including mid-train and tail-end pushers) to defeat the eastbound grade.

Work on reducing the 4.5 percent grade on the Big Hill was not begun until 1907, when a plan incorporating a pair of spiral tunnels and a maximum gradient of 2.2 percent was implemented. Contractors MacDonnell and Gzowski needed a three-foot gauge construction railroad (with at least two narrow-gauge 2–6–0s from the Northwestern Coal and Navigation Company in Alberta), heavy construction equipment, untold quantities of dynamite and a

work force estimated at 1,000 strong to complete the project by the summer of 1909.

The new 8.2-mile assault on the Big Hill doubled the length of the grade but halved the rate of ascent. The danger filled glory days of struggling uphill with just a handful of cars and literally skidding downgrade were over. Just the same, the Big Hill and the spiral tunnels would remain one of the most impressive theatres in Canadian railroading. Double- and triple-headed, eight- and ten-coupled power (and for a brief season, even a small group of home-built 0–6–6–0s) was the order of the day as the CPR forced more and more tonnage through Kicking Horse Pass.

The Canadian Pacific's mountain passage was quickly evolving from a pioneer railroad to a high-capacity mainline. The Big Hill was tamed, fragile wooden trestles gave way to steel replacements and on December 9, 1916, the slide-prone route over Rogers Pass — where a March 1910 snowslide buried a plow train and with it 62 men, and where stiff grades limited freight trains to an average of 950 tons — was abandoned upon completion of the five-mile Connaught Tunnel. The $5.5 million, double-tracked tunnel shortened the route by four and a half miles, eliminated curvature equivalent to seven full circles, as well as four miles of snowsheds and a number of deck-plate girder bridges, and increased tonnage ratings by lowering the summit a total of 450 feet. The CPR was growing up.

Date and location of this photo of Canadian Northern 4–6–0 No. 1261
— outshopped from Alco's Brooks works in 1902 — are unknown.
However, the station is of a design associated with Canadian
Northern lines east of Winnipeg and may aid in pinpointing the
location. *Ontario Archives*

hough the CPR bound the nation from sea to sea, not all Canadians admired the company as a source of national unity and pride. Many resented its western monopoly and hard-line business practices. Anti-CPR sentiments ran high in Manitoba, where right from the start, the CPR antagonized farmers with "excessive" grain rates. From these seeds of discontent sprung the saplings that would quickly mature into a transcontinental rival of the CPR.

Independent branchlines were under construction in Manitoba as early as 1882, but these side-stepped conflict with the CPR by avoiding its territory or, as in the case of the Manitoba & South Western Colonization Railway, selling out to CP. In 1888, the inevitable clash broke out as the provincially sponsored Winnipeg–Emerson and Winnipeg–Portage la Prairie lines challenged the Canadian Pacific on its own turf. While CP built a spur across the right-of-way of the advancing Winnipeg–Emerson Red River Valley Railway in order to provoke a confrontation, the battle royale was at Headingley, where the Portage la Prairie line crossed the CPR main. The stand-off at Headingley would pit the province of Manitoba against the government of Canada, see CPR crews defiantly tear out the competitions' diamond and witness farmers and small-time railroaders face off against the mighty CPR. When the dust settled, the provincial railroad's diamond would be spiked firmly across the

CPR. The CP monopoly would be broken, and as if to pour salt in the CP wounds, Manitoba would turn its lines over to the American-owned Northern Pacific Railway. Furthermore, the province government granted the Northern Pacific and Manitoba Railway a charter to build branchlines — with provincially guaranteed construction bonds — anywhere in Manitoba.

MACKENZIE AND MANN

Taking advantage of its new-found fortune, NP built a line from Morris (on the Emerson line) to Brandon, 145 miles west. However, before any further expansion could be carried out, the alliance went sour and Manitoba needed someone else to build a competitive rail network. The partnership that could and indeed, would take on the CPR was already at work within the boundaries of Manitoba. On January 29, 1896, William MacKenzie and Donald Mann — two names that would become inseparable in the annals of Canadian railroad history — took control of the faltering Lake Manitoba Railway and Canal Co.

Within a year the railroad had been completed from its connection with the Manitoba & North Western (another independent) at Gladstone to its intended terminus at Winnipegosis, 123 miles north. In the meantime, MacKenzie and Mann had also begun construction of the Manitoba and South Eastern Railway a-building southeastward

Canadian Northern Extra 2161 West marches into Dauphin, Manitoba with a lengthy train of wooden boxcars. *Canadian National photo*

from Winnipeg to the U.S. border at Lake of the Woods. Even before its completion, the M&SE turned a profit, cutting and hauling firewood for the Winnipeg market. Several times a week, a mixed train dubbed the "Muskeg Special" clattered over the M&SE, hauling carloads of cordwood (some ·of it borne on flatcars quietly "borrowed" from the CPR) that earned the company an operating surplus of $12,000 in 1898 alone.

THE BIRTH OF THE CNoR

After only two years, MacKenzie and Mann had set more ambitious goals. From a junction with the Winnipegosis line, the Winnipeg Great Northern Railway struck out for Prince Albert and the Manitoba & South Eastern — in direct competition with the CPR — was bound for the lakehead at Port Arthur. In 1899 the holdings were consolidated to form a single company and the Canadian Northern Railway was born.

MacKenzie and Mann were on the move. In 1901, they took over the Northern Pacific's Manitoba lines (which had just been leased by the Manitoba government for 999 years) running from Emerson to Winnipeg, Winnipeg to Portage la Prairie and from Morris to Brandon, with a 51-mile branch to Hartney. The 313-mile, ex-NP network was quickly improved with the construction of 133 miles of connecting lines and feeder branches. Part of the agreement made upon acquiring the NP trackage from the province was that the Canadian Northern never pool traffic or amalgamate with the CPR. There was little danger of that — Canadian Northern was building an empire of its own.

A silver spike driven at Atikokan, Ontario, on December 30, 1902, celebrated completion of the line between Winnipeg and Port Arthur. With an expansive Manitoba network, a direct link to the lakehead and significantly lower freight and grain rates, the Canadian Northern suddenly posed a real threat to the CPR. It would soon become evident that the Canadian Northern was more than just a regional threat — MacKenzie and Mann were building the foundations of a transcontinental railroad.

Intent upon first constructing a prairie system that would support mainlines to the coasts, Canadian Northern spun a web of branchlines that rapidly covered the width and breadth of the prairies. While construction crews spiked rails into such railroad settlements as Ethelbert, Altamont, Glenavon and Zealandia, high-headlighted 2–6–0s, 4–6–0s and 2–8–0s with Canadian Northern embossed on bronze number plates and spelled out across tender flanks, marched across the prairies trailing ever-lengthening strings of wooden box cars, filled to capacity with eastbound grain.

Flying soiled white extra flags, Canadian Northern 4–6–0 No. 172 pauses, presumably with a grain train, at Zealandia, Saskatchewan, 59 miles west of Saskatoon on the line to Calgary, Alberta. *Canadian National photo*

THE CNoR MOVES EAST

Beginning in 1903, the Canadian Northern began infiltration of the east, and within three years had absorbed the Great Northern Railway of Canada and a number of smaller companies. A small but strategic acquisition, the eastern lines gave Canadian Northern trackage from Hawkesbury (on the Ottawa River), east to Quebec City, north to Lake St. John as well as Chicoutimi, Quebec (on the Saguenay River) and, by way of the former Chateauguay and Northern Railway entry into Montreal. This, combined with traffic agreements with the Canada Atlantic Railway and its subsidiary Great Lakes steamers, enabled the Canadian Northern to ship through tonnage from the prairies to the Atlantic.

During this same period, the Canadian Northern established itself in Nova Scotia and Ontario with a combined effort of construction and acquisition. In Nova Scotia, there were lines from Halifax, along the east coast to Yarmouth and cross-province from Bridgewater to Middleton and Port Wade on the Bay of Fundy. Several piecemeal acquisitions in Ontario included the Niagara, St. Catherines and Toronto, a small electrified interurban line on the Niagara Peninsula, but the most significant development was construction of a line north from Toronto toward Sudbury. Opened between Toronto and Parry Sound in November 1906, this was the first leg of an intended Y-shaped mainline that would join at Capreol (near Sudbury) with a line from the east coast and run across northern Ontario to the lakehead.

The original intention of MacKenzie and Mann had been to delay construction of a transcontinental mainline until a prairie system of 5,000 miles had been established. However, competition with the CPR was intensifying and another transcontinental line (the

Canadian Northern 4–6–0 No. 26 leads a short train over the four-span North Saskatchewan River bridge. The photographer captioned this photo "This is the first photo of the first train as she steamed over the bridge and touched the fertile soil of Edmonton . . ." *Public Archives Canada*

NTR/GTP) was on the horizon. MacKenzie and Mann spurned the suggestion of amalgamation or some other form of cooperation with the Grand Trunk and forged ahead with their own plans for an independent railroad from coast to coast.

The Canadian Northern reached Edmonton in 1905, but could not obtain satisfactory government assistance to build further west until 1910. In March 1910, the British Columbia government passed legislation guaranteeing Canadian Northern construction bonds to the tune of $35,000 per mile, as well as tax exemptions, access to crown lands for construction material and free right-of-way through crown land. In return, the C.No.R. would build a line through the mountains to the Pacific coast at Port Mann and establish an ocean terminal and branch line on Vancouver Island. Construction began in October 1910, two and a half years after the Grand Trunk Pacific started building east from Prince Rupert, B.C.

While western construction was stalled at Edmonton, the C.No.R. continued to fill out its branchline network, especially in Saskatchewan and Alberta. In 1906, MacKenzie and Mann scored a victory over the CPR, purchasing the 249-mile Qu'Appelle, Long Lake and Saskatchewan Railroad and Steamboat Company. Previously leased to the CPR, the strategically located north-south line came at a steep price, but netted six million bushels of grain in the first year alone. By 1907, C.No.R.'s prairie-route mileage had swelled to more than 2,800 miles. With Canadian Pacific, Canadian Northern and now Grand Trunk Pacific all competing for prairie traffic, over-building — the results of which would plague the region for three-quarters of a century — was well underway.

Meanwhile, progress was being made in the east. The Toronto leg of the eastern mainline "Y" was completed in 1908 and new mileage was being built or bought in eastern Ontario and Quebec. In 1910 work began on the Toronto–Belleville–Ottawa mainline. Although much of its route had been surveyed and selected, the eastern portion of C.No.R.'s transcontinental mainline became a reality in May 1911, when the federal government guaranteed $35,000-per-mile construction bonds for a 1,050-mile line from Montreal to Port Arthur.

In 1912, Canadian Northern construction crews were blasting their way through the mountains of British Columbia, building east from Port Arthur and working in both directions from Capreol. The Toronto–Ottawa mainline was nearing completion and in Montreal, crews deep within Mount Royal were boring a double-track tunnel that would bring the Canadian Northern downtown. In addition, a 57-mile shortcut from Hawkesbury to the west portal of the Mount Royal tunnel was under construction to ensure that the C.No.R.'s new entry to Montreal would be competitive.

In Minnesota, the Duluth Winnipeg & Pacific (a wholly-owned subsidiary of C.No.R.) was completed between its connection with the Winnipeg–Port Arthur line (just east of Fort Frances, Ontario), and Duluth, giving the C.No.R. a second port on Lake Superior, a major U.S. terminal and access to the rich resource traffic of Minnesota. These were heady years for the Canadian Northern, but the company would never recover from the construction costs, which exceeded estimates several times over.

Incorporating part of the recently purchased Bay of Quinte Railway, the Toronto–Ottawa mainline opened on December 30, 1913, and two days later, on New Year's Day 1914, the last spike of the mainline east of Port Arthur was driven at Little White Otter River. Ballasting and construction of lineside facilities consumed another ten months and in October, regular service commenced between Toronto and Port Arthur. Throughout 1914 new branchlines were opened in Manitoba, Saskatchewan and Alberta and the mainline slowly crept through the mountains.

CROSSING THE CONTINENT

Following the Yellowhead Pass route that Sanford Fleming had recommended to the CPR decades earlier, Canadian Northern followed what observers have labelled the easiest road to the Pacific coast. Nevertheless, the "easy" route confronted railroad builders with the challenge of drilling tunnels totalling

Right: **Canadian Northern train No. 2 bridges the North Saskatchewan River at North Battleford, Sask.** *Public Archives Canada*

thousands of feet, bridging canyons and gorges and spiking miles of railroad to precarious ledges blasted out of sheer canyon walls. Through the Thompson and Fraser river canyons, the C.No.R. had to build on the side rejected by the CPR. As a result, construction costs through Hells Gate soared as high as $350,000 per mile. In the only area where the Canadian Northern could have had a break, the fierce independence of MacKenzie and Mann negated the possibility of joint GTP/C.No.R. trackage through Yellowhead Pass. Instead, the Canadian Northern built 318 miles of duplicate trackage from Edmonton to the west end of Yellowhead Pass at Lucerne, B.C. (where the GTP set out for Prince Rupert).

Where possible, the Canadian Northern kept a respectable distance from the GTP, but for the last 140 miles the two lines ran side by side. The $13 million folly was barely put into service when steel shortages during World War I forced consolidation of the parallel lines and salvage crews were put to work ripping up excess Canadian Northern trackage.

On January 23, 1915, the Canadian Northern finally achieved transcontinental status as the last spike was driven at Basque, B.C., 182 miles east of Port Mann. The occasion was as much cause for a great sigh of relief, as for celebration. During construction of the transcontinental line, MacKenzie and Mann were forced to make repeated appeals for

Section crews struggle to free a wooden Canadian Northern wedge plow and a pair of 2–8–0's stalled on February 1, 1916 in a drift at Milepost 1 on the Carlyle Subdivision in southern Saskatchewan. *Foote Collection, Manitoba Archives*

In a scene little changed from the Canadian Northern days, CN boxcab electric No. 9103 (ex-Can. Nor. No. 603) and four wooden coaches ease into Vertu, Quebec with inbound commuter train #310. *Philip R. Hastings*

government assistance and had worn out their welcome on world money markets. The Canadian Northern was wallowing in a sea of debt from which it would never emerge.

Earlier commitments to the province of British Columbia forced the Canadian Northern to continue its half-hearted construction of several branchlines on Vancouver Island. The 51-mile line from Victoria to Kinsol was not completed until 1920, while the remaining lines were finished between 1923 and 1928 . . . under a new flag.

THE MOUNT ROYAL TUNNEL

As a private entity, the Canadian Northern was in its final days when the Mount Royal Tunnel — an ambitious project undertaken in more prosperous times — saw its first regular train. Complete government takeover was imminent, when at 08:15, October 21, 1918, Canadian Northern boxcab electric 601 — drawing current from a 2,400-volt overhead catenary — led a seven-car passenger train

through the 16,315-foot, $12.3 million, electrified double-track Mount Royal Tunnel. A final tribute to the accomplishments of MacKenzie and Mann, the Mount Royal Tunnel was an impressive piece of railroad. The line was electrified from the Tunnel Terminal Station in downtown Montreal, through the tunnel and beyond to Lazard (now Val Royal) and Cartierville, Quebec — a distance of 8.2 miles. The tunnel operation was all-electric, with a half-dozen four-motor 80-ton boxcabs (built in 1914, by Canadian General Electric in Peterborough, Ontario) handling through passenger trains between Montreal and Lazard (where steam locomotives took over), as well as suburban trains to Lazard and Cartierville (at the end of a 0.9-mile stub-end branch off the mainline).

The tunnel, the electrification, in place between Montreal–Val Royal/Cartierville and Deux Montagnes and even the 1914–built boxcab electrics remain in operation, but 60 days after the 601 (now CN 6711) hauled the first public passenger train through the Mount Royal Tunnel, the Canadian Northern Railway would be stripped of its corporate identity.

THE DEATH OF THE CNoR

In response to government pressure, MacKenzie and Mann, along with their top company officers, resigned on September 6, 1918 and were replaced with a government appointed board of directors. The government now held 310,000 of 600,000 Canadian Northern Railway shares. Under federal direction, the Canadian Northern soon assumed control of the Canadian Government Railways, which included the National Transcontinental's Eastern Division, the Intercolonial Railway, the Prince Edward Island Railway and eight short lines in New Brunswick. On December 20, 1918, the death-knell tolled for the Canadian Northern as the government issued an Order-in-Council proclaiming that the amalgamated Canadian Government Railways and Canadian Northern Railway would bear "the collective and descriptive designation" of the Canadian National Railways. Although the merger was not legally consummated until January 20, 1923, the Canadian Northern identity was buried and consolidation of the two systems began on March 31, 1919.

THE GRAND TRUNK MOVES WEST

There is evidence that in the years prior to the incorporation of the Canadian Pacific Railway, the Canadian government — under Sir John A. Macdonald — approached the Grand Trunk with a proposition to build the railroad to the Pacific. Among the GTR's reasons for declining the offer was the government's insistence that an all-Canadian route be followed rather than the Grand Trunk's preferred route through Chicago. (This same policy was responsible for James J. Hill's departure from the original CPR executive committee and the subsequent rivalry between the CP and Hill's Great Northern.) Reluctance to build a line north of Superior would lock the Grand Trunk out of the Canadian west until after the turn of the century.

Before long, the GTR had realized that it could no longer ignore the west and began to explore various methods of extending itself. By the early 1900s, Canadian Pacific had turned down Grand Trunk offers of generous rental payments and reciprocal trackage rights over all GTR lines in the east, in exchange for run-

As evidenced by this scene on the Grand Trunk Pacific, the dawn of "mechanized" track laying speeded up construction and eased the burden on the backs of railroad builders. *Canadian National photo*

ning rights over the CPR from North Bay to the west. Subsequent attempts to strike a co-operative agreement (read takeover in some quarters) and form a single east–west system with the Canadian Northern were unsuccessful — even though the federal government desperately wanted the GTR and C.No.R. to cooperate.

THE GTPR AND THE NTR

In 1903, the government and the Grand Trunk reluctantly came to terms, giving birth to the Grand Trunk Pacific Railway and the National Transcontinental Railway. Under the terms of the agreement the Grand Trunk Pacific Rail-way — a wholly-owned GTR subsidiary — would build (with federal assistance), own and operate the Winnipeg–Prince Rupert, B.C., Western Division of the National Trans-continental, while the NTR's Moncton, New Brunswick–Winnipeg Eastern Division would be government-owned and upon completion would be leased to the GTP for 50 years. The initial seven years would be rent-free, but thereafter, the GTP would pay a fee based upon three percent of the Eastern Division's construction costs.

Surveyors began blazing the path of the National Transcontinental in 1903, and by 1905, the Grand Trunk Pacific was building across the prairies. A year later, construction of the Moncton–Quebec City–Winnipeg main-line of the Eastern Division was underway. As expected, work progressed rapidly on the prairies. By the fall of 1907, the rail gangs were nearing Saskatchewan and eastbound work trains were lifting grain as they returned to Winnipeg for supplies. The Eastern Division lagged far behind. The first portion of the NTR to see regular traffic, the 80–mile section between Hervey Junction and Quebec City opened in the summer of 1909 — about the same time the first GTP train reached Edmonton.

FROM EDMONTON TO PRINCE RUPERT

While the Grand Trunk Pacific inaugurated services on the prairie, contractors were at work on the GTP line from Edmonton to the Pacific coast at Prince Rupert, B.C. Facing one of the toughest railroad-building jobs on the continent, contractors worked east from Prince Rupert and west from Edmonton. Supplies were forwarded by wagon train in summer and sledge in winter. During the winter of 1910–1911, horsedrawn sledges hauled almost 30,000 tons of supplies, including several large steam shovels and a 60-ton steam locomotive. Wherever rivers showed even a hint of naviga-

bility, fleets of steamboats, sternwheelers, scows and canoes were pressed into service to deliver supplies to remote work camps. Boats often had to be cabled or winched through the most treacherous waters. Trips that took as long as eight days upstream could be covered in as little as 14 hours returning downstream. It was dangerous work and it is said that the Skeena River claimed 50 lives in just the first season.

The GTP route to the Pacific coast ran afoul of almost every obstacle imaginable. Muskegs were mattressed with corduroy log beds; deposits of gumbo clay caused slides and had to be excavated and filled with rock. Bridges — some of the longest and highest in the land — were built over canyons, ravines and boiling rivers. Tunnels were numerous. At Mile 44 a 1,600-foot tunnel was drilled through a mountainside plagued by avalanches and rock slides and at Kitselas crews tunnelled through 2,200 feet of granite. On the Skeena section east of Prince Rupert, tunnels totalled 8,886 feet. Miles of railroad had to be carved out of solid rock; one contract consumed 10,000,000 pounds of explosives and included a 6,660–foot rock cut that took 26 months to finish. Even the names sounded forbidding: Hole in the Wall, Sealy Gulch, Snaring and Kitwonga. The first contracts were let in 1908. In six years the contractors succeeded in building a remarkable mountain railroad that topped the Continental Divide in Yellowhead Pass at an elevation of 3,717 feet above sea level (versus CPR's Kicking Horse Pass crossing at 5,326 feet), maintaining a maximum gradient of one percent all the way to the coast. When the line

On an unknown date in 1915, Grand Trunk Pacific 4-6-0 No. 614 stomps out of Prince Rupert, B.C. with a nine-car train for Winnipeg. Built by MLW in 1910, the 614 would soon become Canadian National No. 1437 and would survive in CNR employ until 1954. *Public Archives Canada*

to Prince Rupert was opened in 1914, the Grand Trunk Pacific could hang a whopping 1,876 tons behind the tender of an average freight engine — more than twice the tonnage ratings allowed over the CPR's crossing of the Continental Divide — spiral tunnels and all.

BUILDING THE NTR EASTERN DIVISION

Meanwhile, contractors building the NTR Eastern Division were doing battle with the muskeg, sinkholes, clay belts and swamps of northern Quebec and Ontario. Sinkholes swallowed trainload after trainload of fill and muskeg stretched unbroken for miles. In some places, retaining the completed trackage was as much a problem as the construction. With no load upon it and little warning, a recently completed 1,000-foot steel bridge over the Okidodasik River on the Quebec–Ontario border simply rolled over on its side — the victim of a clay slide.

Nature was hard on the Eastern Division contractors, but it was the railroad builders who were ruthless with the NTR. Construction costs were falsified, prices inflated and profits were padded — often by an additional 40 to 50 percent. A royal commission investigating dishonest practices during construction of the NTR estimated that approximately $70 million, or 43 percent of the $169 million price tag on the Eastern Division, had been wasted or lost to unscrupulous contractors. When the last spike on the National Transcontinental Eastern Division was completed, Canadian taxpayers were handed a bill $100 million

higher than the original estimates.

Completed under a cloud of political controversy, the National Transcontinental was ready for regular service in 1915, but to add insult to injury, the Grand Trunk Pacific reneged on its promise to lease and operate the Eastern Division. As a result, the National Transcontinental joined the Intercolonial Railway and the PEI Railway as part of the Canadian Government Railways. The CGR began scheduled service between Quebec City and Superior Junction on June 1, 1915, extended trains to Winnipeg by August and inaugurated Moncton–Quebec City service in November. In addition, the Grand Trunk Pacific branch built between the NTR mainline at Superior Junction and Fort William was leased in perpetuity, giving the CGR an outlet to the lakehead.

THE QUEBEC BRIDGE

Although the NTR was technically complete, there was a 3,239-foot gap in the Moncton–Winnipeg mainline. At Quebec City, NTR traffic was ferried across the St. Lawrence River, in sight of the ill-starred, incomplete Quebec Bridge. First chartered in 1887, the Quebec Bridge, a monstrous cantilever structure, was only partially completed when, on the morning of August 29, 1907, the entire south anchor arm and cantilever buckled, groaned and collapsed — carrying scores of workers to their deaths as 9,000 tons of steel crashed to the St. Lawrence floor. Accounts differ, but the death toll — pegged between 70 and 84 men —

still ranks the Quebec Bridge Disaster as one of the worst accidents in Canadian history.

A second Quebec Bridge was begun in 1914, 65 feet upstream from the original location. On September 11, 1916, a 640-foot span, built to connect the completed north and south cantilevers of the new bridge, was floated upstream and slowly raised into position. At 10:50, success within grasp, a cruciform support on the southwest corner of the lifting apparatus fractured. With the balance upset, the span plunged into the St. Lawrence. The incident claimed another 13 lives and the 640-foot gap in the NTR mainline would remain unbridged for more than a year. A replacement span was constructed during the summer of 1917 and the entire maneuver was repeated between September 17 and 20. At 16:00 hours, September 20, 1917, the permanent suspension bars were secured and the Quebec Bridge was complete — at a cost of over $21.6 million and nearly 100 lives. The first train crossed the bridge on October 17. Regular service was not inaugurated until December 3, 1917, with the passage of a CGR freight headed by brand new Montreal Locomotive Works 2–8–2 No. 2900 (later CNR 3300).

FINANCIAL WOES

With the Quebec Bridge now in place and the CGR/GTP in full operation, Canada's three transcontinental railroads were physically established. However, only the CPR was financially secure. The Canadian Northern had less than a year of independence remaining and in the spring of 1919, the Grand Trunk would default on its Grand Trunk Pacific securities. The GTP came under government control on March 7, 1919 — three days before all operations of the bankrupt road were scheduled to grind to a halt. Originally the responsibility of the minister of railways and canals, the GTP was placed under Canadian National management on July 12, 1920.

In the fight to preserve its own independence the financially crippled Grand Trunk set itself on a self-destructive course that effectively thrust the company into the government's hands. On May 21, 1920, a government Board of Management took over operation of the 7,957-mile Grand Trunk system, including the company's 1,164-mile U.S. subsidiaries. While the GTP was quickly absorbed into the newly formed crown corporation — Canadian National Railways — the Grand Trunk proper retained its separate identity during drawn-out arbitration proceedings regarding the government acquisition. On January 30, 1923, the Grand Trunk Railway was formally incorporated into the Canadian National Railways system.

GROWTH OF THE CNR

From its humble beginnings as an informal label for the amalgamated Canadian Northern and Canadian Government Railways, the

Bottom: Although the Grand Trunk Pacific inherited a fleet of hand-me-down engines from its eastern parent, GTP was also provided with new power, such as 2–8–0 No. 821, one of 60 MLW-built Consolidations purchased for the GTP in 1911–1912. The 821 became CNR No. 2698 and was retired in October 1959. *Canadian National photo*

Canadian National Railways grew — in five short years — into the largest railroad system in the world. On January 30, 1923, the Canadian National Railways System consisted of 22,646 route-miles of trackage, with ancestral roots in no less than 221 individual railway companies — including Canada's first railway, the Champlain and St. Lawrence. Under the Canadian National flag, the identities of predecessor roads were quickly lost. However, for legal reasons, U.S. subsidiaries of the Canadian Northern and the Grand Trunk retained corporate individuality. Thus, long after the parent companies disappeared in the CN melting pot, the Duluth, Winnipeg & Pacific, Central Vermont, Grand Trunk (GTEL-GTR New England lines) and Grand Trunk Western (GTR lines in Michigan, Illinois, Indiana and Wisconsin) lived on.

The operating statistics of the 22,646-mile railroad were overwhelming, rostering 3,265 locomotives, 3,363 cars in passenger service, 124,648 freight cars, 6,544 company service cars, and posting a payroll of 102,454 employees. But the system's inherited debt, estimated at a staggering $1,311,448,713, went beyond the limits of imagination.

Sir Henry Worth Thornton, a well-educated railroader who had risen from an 1894 start with the Pennsylvania Railroad to presidential assistant on the Long Island Railroad and then to general manager of England's Great Eastern Railway, took office in January 1923 as the first Canadian National president. Observers deemed it an unenviable position, akin to being appointed captain of a sinking ship.

Nevertheless, Thornton mastered the challenge — pushing the CNR to an operating surplus of $18 million in the first year and setting the railroad on a course that would, after decades of long hard work, make the Canadian National a respected and profitable operation.

Bearing testimony to GTP's easy crossing of the Continental Divide, GTP 4–6–2 No. 1112 singlehandedly works an 11-car passenger train through Jasper Park, Alberta. *Public Archives Canada*

Northern Alberta's unique policy of assigning 2–10–0's to passenger trains is illustrated as train #7 leaves Edmonton for Waterways behind CLC-built Decapod 52 on July 17, 1959. *Paterson-George Collection*

s the railroads civilized the west, they also opened new frontiers to the north. Visionaries viewed the completed lines not as an end but as the means to penetrate further into the hinterland. Construction of the Canadian Northern fired long-simmering dreams of a railroad from the Manitoba prairie to Hudson Bay. Edmonton was seen as a perfect stepping-off point for railroads reaching into northern Alberta. However, Canada's northernmost railroad was built, not from some windswept prairie "end of steel," but from an Alaskan harbour, on the heels of the Klondike Gold Rush.

THE WHITE PASS & YUKON RAILWAY

Exercising three separate charters, the White Pass & Yukon built from the coastal harbour at Skagway, Alaska, to Whitehorse, Yukon — 110.7 rugged rail-miles inland. Construction began at Skagway on May 28, 1898, as crews laid a three-foot gauge railroad straight up the centre of Broadway Street. Two hundred and sixty-seven days later construction gangs spiked rails over the 2,885-foot summit of White Pass and into British Columbia. Behind them lay 20.4 miles of $100,000-plus per mile twisting and climbing railroad — most of it carved out of solid rock, at an ascending rate of 3.9 percent. Ahead lay 90 miles more of hostile terrain, but by this time a second crew — working south from Whitehorse — was helping to close the gap.

On July 29, 1900, the advancing railheads met at Carcross (originally known as Caribou Crossing), Yukon Territory, and a gold spike was driven to celebrate the occasion. Scheduled service began between Skagway and Whitehorse on August 15, but the gold rush that had inspired the railway was waning. During the first few years, passengers and mining activity provided enough traffic to keep the WP&Y's fleet of Brooks, Baldwin and Grant 2–6–0s and 2–8–0s (and even a three-truck Climax and a BLW 4–4–0) busy and black ink on the ledgers. But by 1913 the road stopped paying dividends and in 1918 it underwent financial reorganization. In that same year, a short branch from Macrae (near Whitehorse) to Pueblo was abandoned after opening only eight years earlier. Traffic bottomed out between 1931–1935, when yearly tonnage remained at or below 12,000 tons.

Business picked up enough in the pre-war years to justify acquisition of a pair of brand new Baldwin 2–8–2s. With the outbreak of World War II, the WP&Y was transformed overnight from an unremarked Klondike survivor to a vital northern artery. For the first time in its existence, the White Pass was

Although traffic levels dropped far below the wartime records, the WP&Y prospered in pushed to the limit, moving outbound Yukon resources and inbound supplies for construction of the Alaska highway. During the first nine months of 1942, the WP&Y moved a record 67,496 tons. The record would not last a year.

WORLD WAR II AND THE WP&Y

Because of the line's strategic importance, the United States government leased the WP&Y for the duration of the war. On 00:01 October 1, 1942, the road effectively became the U.S. army's 770th Railway Operating Battalion, part of the Military Railway Service. To supplement the WP&Y's overworked stable of ten locomotives, the M.R.S. brought with it an assorted collection of narrow-gauge engines ranging from pairs of Silverton Northern 2–8–0s, East Tennessee & Western North Carolina 4–6–0s and Colorado & Southern (ex-Denver South Park and Pacific) Consolidations, to seven Denver & Rio Grande Western K-28 class outside-framed 2–8–2s and 11 new U.S. Army 2–8–2s, built by Baldwin for service in Iran, but diverted to the Yukon and converted from metre-gauge to WP&Y's 3-foot gauge. The army also boosted the White Pass freight car fleet from 83 to 341 cars and supplied additional train crews and other manpower.

In 1943, with such a massive shot in the arm, the White Pass was able to force an unbelievable 281,962 tons — more than ten times the average annual tonnage of the pre-war years — over its 110.7-mile line. All of this tonnage was moved despite one of the worst winters in memory. It was a season that kept ancient Cooke rotary snowplows on two-hour call, froze engines to the rails and saw a derailment on the 215-foot-high cantilever bridge over Dead Horse Gulch. There were blizzards and gale-force winds that closed the line for ten days in February and stranded near-starving train crews until bulldozers could break through. Railroading has seen precious few moments more dramatic than the war efforts of the White Pass.

GATEWAY TO THE YUKON

After the war the White Pass reverted to its original status as a mining and frontier railroad. The army pulled out, the war department Mikes were honourably discharged and immediately hired by the WP&Y. The orphaned hand-me-downs imported from the south were shoved onto back tracks at Skagway and stood rusting in silent testament to the war years that would go down in history as the White Pass's finest hour.

A U.S. Army 2–8–2 and WP&Y 2–8–0 (cut in ahead of the baggage car) doublehead a mixed train over Dead Horse Gulch Viaduct during World War II. *Canadian Pacific Collection*

peacetime. Revenues were sufficient to finance the 1947 purchase of a pair of oil-burning, low-drivered, 128,000-pound Baldwin 2–8–2s numbered 72 and 73 — identical to WP&Y 70–71, delivered by Baldwin in 1938 and 1939.

With a "fair weather" rating of 140 tons apiece for the 3.9 percent assault on White Pass, Nos. 70–73 were — in the opinion of WP&Y men — the finest narrow-gauge engines ever built. The oil-burning Baldwins were the backbone of the post-war White Pass fleet, supplemented by surviving war department 2–8–2s and supported by a pair of indispensible 77-ton Cooke rotaries built in 1900.

Sustaining itself on a steady diet of outbound resource tonnage, inbound staples of Yukon life and a respectable, if not profitable, passenger trade, the White Pass — Mikes, rotaries, open-platform wooden coaches and all — may not have realized its dreams of building deep into the Yukon, but it unquestionably fulfilled and maintained its original slogan — "Gateway to the Yukon."

THE ALGOMA CENTRAL RAILWAY

While the White Pass pursued its dreams of Klondike gold, an industrialist a half a continent away chartered a railroad to exploit northern Ontario reserves of iron ore and vast stands of timber. The less glamorous but more stable ambitions of Francis Clergue resulted in the 1899 birth of the Algoma Central Railway, authorized to build north from Sault Ste. Marie, Ontario. The primary goal of the ACR was to reach iron ore deposits at Helen Mine, although in 1901, in a fit of over-ambition, Clergue tagged "Hudson Bay" on the end of the company name and set his sights on the far-north ocean outlet.

To take advantage of the nearby ore, Clergue established the Algoma Iron, Nickel, and Steel Company at Sault Ste. Marie in 1902. One hundred and forty miles of rugged terrain separated the steel mill from the iron ore. While the railroad built its mainline north, it also built a short branch from Helen Mine to

Michipicoten Harbour on Lake Superior. Algoma Central steamships then expedited movement of the ore between mine and blast furnace until the railroad linked Sault Ste. Marie and Helen Mine in 1912.

The grandly named but financially strapped Algoma Central & Hudson Bay Railway was completed between Sault Ste. Marie and Hearst, Ontario (where it connected with the mainline of the National Transcontinental) in 1914. It would advance no further. The empty promise of "Hudson Bay" would vanish from common usage but linger in the road's formal title until 1965. The financial road to Hearst had been as rocky as the terrain traversed by the 296-mile mainline and the figures inked on the bottom line of AC&HB balance sheets were red.

Compromise was a way of life on the Algoma Central and the forced frugality was reflected in the company's locomotive roster from day one. Operations began, not with the traditional brand-new custom-built engines, but with four

hand-me-down, ex-Lehigh Valley 4–6–0s and a group of used Burlington 0–4–0s. The first new power on the AC&HB arrived in the form of four Baldwin Consolidations and a pair of Canadian Locomotive Company 0–6–0s. The acquisition was complemented with the purchase of two ex-Iron Range & Huron Bay 4–8–0s (a rare wheel arrangement north of the border). As if to celebrate its completion, the AC&HB splurged in 1912 — splitting an order for five "passenger" 4–6–0s and 15 drag service 2–8–0s between Montreal Locomotive Works and Canadian Locomotive Company. Seventeen years later, on the eve of the Great Depression, Canadian Locomotive Company delivered a pair of beetle-browed, 338,800-pound 2–10–2s that would be the road's last new steam power. The tonnage boom brought on by World War II sent the Algoma Central back to the used locomotive market and buyers returned to Sault Ste. Marie with 17 aged Mikes of Minneapolis & St. Louis, Virginian and Wabash lineage.

Algoma Central 4–8–0 No. 3 eases a mixed consist over the Belleview trestle, one of the largest wooden trestles in Canada. *Ontario Archives*

Coal smoke hung heavy over Agawa Canyon as the AC&HB's variegated fleet hauled enough pulpwood and lumber, iron ore and finished Algoma steel to keep a shine on interchange tracks at the "Soo," Franz, Oba and Hearst, and, more importantly, to bankroll the upgrading of the railroad and banish red ink from the company books. The Algoma Central would have a future as solid as the granite walls of Agawa Canyon.

THE TEMISKAMING & NORTHERN ONTARIO RAILWAY

Anxious to develop the northern reaches of the province and wary of the corruption and fraud that plagued other "government" railroads (particularly the Intercolonial and the National Transcontinental), the provincial government of Ontario sought to build its own railway into the northland. In 1902, the province appointed a committee to oversee the building and operation of the Temiskaming & Northern Ontario Railway, a colonization and development railway stretching from North Bay, Ontario (a division point on the CPR's transcontinental line as well as the northernmost point on the Grand Trunk) to the shores of James Bay.

Construction got underway in 1903 and within months, the T&NO's impact on the north exceeded all expectations. Working the southeast shore of Long Lake in search of timber suitable for use as ties, T&NO contractors J. H. McKinley and Ernest Darragh stumbled instead upon rich deposits of silver. Their find — 103 miles north of North Bay, at what is now Cobalt, Ontario — triggered a mining boom and revealed that the Temiskaming & Northern Ontario had struck the heart of one of the richest regions of mineral wealth in the province. Silver bullion stacked on the open baggage carts was a common sight on station platforms and by 1913, ore accounted for ten percent of local freight. Silver shipped out of Cobalt on the T&NO between 1904 and 1915 totalled $122,750,000 and the railroad profited further from royalties on silver veins located beneath its tracks.

Regular service between North Bay and New Liskeard was instituted in 1905 and T&NO trains on the 112-mile run were burdened with settlers, prospectors, mining equipment and supplies. A year later trains were running to Englehart, and by 1909, the T&NO reached Cochrane, 252 miles north of North Bay.

Located on the mainline of the still a-building National Transcontinental, Cochrane would be

T&NO 4-6-0 No. 128, built by CLC in 1909, leads a passenger train out of Englehart, Ont. in 1917. *Public Archives Canada*

the source of considerable revenue for the T&NO. Trainloads of construction supplies for the federally sponsored railroad rolled into Cochrane on the T&NO and with the opening of the east–west main, the NTR interchanged substantial southbound traffic to the line.

The T&NO followed the riches of the region, building branchlines from Cobalt to the mining district at Kerr Lake, from Englehart to Charlton, east from Porquis Junction to a connection with Abitibi Pulp and Paper's company railroad out of Iroquois Falls; from Earlton to Elk Lake and, following the discovery of gold, from Porquis to South Porcupine and Timmins. Somewhat out of character, the railroad even acquired a Cobalt–

Hailcybury–New Liskeard interurban line known as the Nipissing Central Railway. True to its purpose, the Temiskaming & Northern Ontario opened up the north, and indeed became an indispensible part of everyday life. Wayfreights, local passenger and mixed trains — generally powered by CLC or MLW-built Ten Wheelers — were the lifeblood of on-line communities. The trains brought in heating coal and mail, foodstuffs and merchandise from the big city mail-order catalogues. Drag freights tramped through town with ore from the mines and miles of raw and finished forest products and the *Cobalt Special* offered through cars and overnight service — via the Grand Trunk — to Toronto.

Blistering newspaper editorials attacked the railroad's exorbitant freight rates. But when the great forest fires of 1911, 1916 and 1922 destroyed Cochrane, Matheson, Porcupine, Haileybury and scores of smaller settlements, T&NO's regular trains and hastily organized rescue trains saved thousands of lives in the path of the rapidly advancing fire storms. Railroaders were the heroes of the hour. There were numerous accounts of train crews braving walls of fire to reach isolated communities; of rescue trains that shuttled in and out of burning towns until passage was impossible and of trains — with refugees crammed aboard T&NO coaches, boxcars and even flatcars — negotiating heat-twisted rails and burning ties in their flight to safety.

When the fires had passed, leaving near total devastation in many towns, the T&NO acknowledged its moral commitments as a "citizen" of the north. Relief trains brought in tons of food, clothing, bedding and supplies. The T&NO gave free tickets to fire victims, did sombre duty transporting remains and offered free telegraph services to relay news — good or bad — to relatives.

The fires only tempered the northern spirit; new life rose from the ashes. The T&NO now eyed expansion into new frontiers. While pondering the prospects of the oft-proposed James Bay extension, the Temiskaming & Northern Ontario activated the dormant charters of subsidiary Nipissing Central to build east, beyond the Ontario boundary to the gold and copper mining fields at Rouyn/Noranda, Quebec. The 60-mile line from the mainline at Swastika, Ontario to Rouyn/Noranda was completed in 1928, while the on-again–off-again line from Cochrane to the proposed James Bay terminus at Moosonee was faltering midway to the Bay.

The Depression put an end to the indecision surrounding the completion of the James Bay extension. Continued construction kept the men working and the railroad was pushed with renewed conviction. The line was completed in 1931, opened with a triple-spike ceremony at Moosonee, Ontario on July 15, 1932 — 30 years after the government formally commissioned the Temiskaming & Northern Ontario.

Moosonee failed to achieve its idealized

status as an ocean port, but the Temiskaming & Northern Ontario was every bit the northern lifeline its promoters envisioned it to be. In 1946, the T&NO was re-christened the Ontario Northland, a more definitive identity for the railroad that stretched from North Bay to Moosonee — and one that eliminated its initials being confused with Southern Pacific's subsidiary the Texas and New Orleans.

THE HUDSON BAY RAILWAY

Ontario's line was not the only railroad to Hudson Bay. Manitoba's efforts to build a railroad to a prairie ocean port on Hudson Bay predated the incorporation of the Canadian Pacific Railway. Indeed, Manitobans had chartered more than a half dozen still-born railroads to the sub-Arctic tidewater before the CPR had spiked down even a mile of its prairie mainline. Nevertheless, the prairie railroad to the Bay was still a dream in 1909, when the Temiskaming & Northern Ontario reached Cochrane on its provincially sponsored drive to a northern ocean port. By this time, the voices of the newly formed provinces of Saskatchewan and Alberta had joined the call for a prairie ocean outlet and the federal government was put under increasing pressure to provide one.

While controversy raged over whether the port should be established at Port Nelson or Churchill, the minister of railways and canals turned the first sod of the railroad to Hudson Bay in September 1910, at The Pas, Manitoba — end of steel on the Canadian Northern's pre-empted road to the Bay. Those with any knowledge of shipping raised a furious outcry against the selection of Port Nelson, citing its

Top: Brakemen decorate the rooftops of wooden Canadian Northern boxcars as a diminutive 4–4–0 pilots a mixed freight over the wobbly trackage of the Hudson Bay Railway about 1914. *Manitoba Archives*

The second section of train #418 rolls into North Bay, Ont. behind elephant-eared 2–8–2 No. 306 on May 12, 1948. *Paterson-George Collection*

inadequacies as a seaport, but the government turned a deaf ear and forged ahead. As the railroad pushed north, ships sailed men and materials into Port Nelson to begin work on the terminal and port facilities. The initial journey from Halifax to Port Nelson in the summer of 1913 forecast the shape of things to come. Two ships were lost, another had to return without unloading its cargo and winter set in before the crews were fully established. Undaunted, the government proceeded with construction that included a 5,000-foot-long, 4,000-foot-wide, man-made island connected to the mainland by a 17-span steel bridge.

At the close of 1917, shortages created by World War I forced all work on the Hudson Bay Railroad to a halt. With the Port Nelson bridge in place, the island partially completed and the railhead advanced to Kettle Rapids — Mile 333 — the Hudson Bay Railway was in limbo once again.

The construction contract was cancelled and the Canadian National Railways assumed operation of the existing trackage in October, 1919. While the government reassessed the practicality of completing the HBR, a bi-monthly mixed train, affectionately labelled the "Muskeg Special," worked the line from The Pas to Pikwitonei at Mile 214. Rumblings that the Hudson Bay Railway would not be completed created an uproar in the west. The pro-HBR On to the Bay Association ensured that the railroad became an election issue. In 1926, the barely re-elected government of Mackenzie King committed itself to completion of the Hudson Bay Railway. Monies were allotted to rebuild the existing trackage and an English engineer finally convinced the government to abandon Port Nelson in favour of Churchill. Despite the need to build an additional 75 miles of railroad, the move to Churchill created estimated savings of more than $12.5 million, halved completion time to three years and lowered the forecast cost of upkeep by more

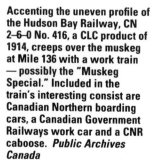

Accenting the uneven profile of the Hudson Bay Railway, CN 2–6–0 No. 416, a CLC product of 1914, creeps over the muskeg at Mile 136 with a work train — possibly the "Muskeg Special." Included in the train's interesting consist are Canadian Northern boarding cars, a Canadian Government Railways work car and a CNR caboose. *Public Archives Canada*

than $1 million per year.

Through the late 1920s a work force of 3,000 pushed the railroad through northern Manitoba, beyond the tree line and over the tundra to the Hudson Bay tidewater at Churchill. Labouring through the bitterly cold winters, they built skeleton track on a corduroy mattress of brush laid on top of the snow. During summers plagued by black flies, the trackage was jacked up, ballasted, straightened and graded. Work trains lurched over unstable skeleton track as the railhead moved north — and as always, muskegs swallowed immeasurable quantities of fill. The steel reached

little more than three months a year. The value of this port, capable of handling only a fraction of the prairies' export grain, would remain controversial for generations. The port of Churchill, the coveted prairie port — a tundra-bound ocean outlet linked to the prairies by a 500-mile steel rail umbilical cord — was nevertheless a reality.

ALBERTA'S RAILWAYS

The people and governments of the prairie provinces have traditionally taken an active and very vocal stand on railroad affairs. For the most part, though, railroads were considered to be a federal responsibility and the prairie governments preferred to keep it that way. In a break with this tradition, the provincial government of Alberta got into the railroad business in the 1920s.

In 1920, the Province of Alberta acquired Winnipeg railway contractor J. D. MacArthur Company's three independent short lines running north and northwest of Edmonton. The Edmonton Dunvegan & British Columbia (running from Edmonton to the Peace River district) and the Central Canada Railway (running north and west from the ED&BC to Peace River Crossing) were initially leased from MacArthur and contracted to the CPR for operation. The third MacArthur line, the Alberta and Great Waterways (running north from the ED&BC at Carbondale — just north of Edmonton), was purchased and government-operated by the Department of Railways and Telephones.

During the 1920s, the government sponsored further construction. The ED&BC was pushed west toward its eventual terminus at Dawson Creek, British Columbia. The Central Canada was extended to Hines Creek, Alberta; the A&GW reached its chartered terminus at Waterways (282.9 rail miles north of Carbon-

Churchill on March 29, 1929 and the last spike — a plain iron one, wrapped in tinfoil from a tobacco package — was driven home on April 3.

The line was capable of handling light traffic by the fall of 1929 and a symbolic 1,800-pound shipment of grain bound for Europe was dispatched from Churchill before winter. Port facilities, including a 2.5-million bushel grain elevator, were completed during the summer of 1931. On September 1, the Farnworth, a freighter of British registry, docked at Churchill to take on the prairie port's first real shipment of grain. Severe Arctic winters would limit the shipping season out of Churchill to

Top Left: **This photo was probably taken at Saskatoon, Sask., where the first grain train to Churchill originated on August 26, 1936. No. 2163, an ex-Canadian Northern 2–8–0, was scrapped 30 years later, in September 1961.** *Public Archives Canada*

dale) and the government chartered and built the 26.5-mile Pembina Valley Railway from the ED&BC mainline at Busby to Barrhead. The province also purchased the previously leased ED&BC and CCR, terminated Canadian Pacific's operation contract and in November 1926, signed a deal with the CNR. Canadian National operated the provincial lines for just over two years.

NORTHERN ALBERTA RAILWAYS

On January 29, 1929, the Government of Alberta consolidated its four railroads under the descriptive corporate flag of the Northern Alberta Railways, owned by Canadian National and Canadian Pacific in equal partnership. The NAR's joint ownership manifested itself in everything from station designs to motive power. The Northern Alberta roster was consistently filled out with engines leased simultaneously from CN and CP, but the NAR purchased only one secondhand steam locomotive from its co-owners: Canadian Pacific G2 class 4–6–2 No. 2563 — an MLW graduate of 1909 — became NAR 161 in June, 1947.

The NAR's own engines reflected the partnership, with CN-style brass number plates hung beneath their headlights and CP-inspired cab numbers and tender stencilling. However, the lettering on number plates and tender flanks clearly spelled out NORTHERN ALBERTA and the railroad flaunted its individuality. The only company-owned locomotive to sport a trailing truck was that lone ex-CPR G2; Decapods were regularly assigned to passenger service; passenger equipment was painted in non-conventional blue and timetables posted a mixed train with sleeping car accommodations.

THE PACIFIC GREAT EASTERN RAILWAY

Like its eastern neighbour, the province of British Columbia also got into the railroad business. In 1918, the provincial government of British Columbia took over the Pacific Great Eastern Railway, a maverick outfit that — quite literally — ran from nowhere to nowhere.

Begun in 1907, as the Howe Sound, Pemberton Valley & Northern, the PGE had faltered in its bid to build from Vancouver, B.C., to connection with the Grand Trunk Pacific at Fort George, British Columbia (now Prince George). When the province moved in, 176 miles of track had been laid north of Squamish (the original southern terminus of the HSPV&N) and only 13 miles of the North Vancouver–Squamish line were in place. By 1921, the province had managed to extend the PGE north to Quesnel — 347 miles from

Squamish — but the line from North Vancouver was stalled, and abandoned in 1928.

For more than 30 years, the PGE's only link with the outside world were freight car-carrying barges and passenger ferries to and from Vancouver, B.C. and Seattle and Bellingham, Washington. PGE 2–8–0s and handsome — but lightweight — Mikados did battle with arduous 2.2 percent grades. The trains clung precariously to canyon walls and crept over spindly wooden trestles to ferry supplies to remote outposts in the B.C. interior and bring resource traffic, primarily forest products, back to Squamish. Physically disconnected from the rest of the nation's railroads, the lonely but spectacular PGE was variously labelled the "Please Go Easy," "Province's Greatest Expense" and the "Prince George Eventually" and was widely known as "the road from nowhere to nowhere."

THE GREAT NORTHERN IN CANADA

Just as Canadians looked north to new frontiers, so did the Americans. Several U.S. railroads made inroads into Canada. By the early 1900s no fewer than ten American railroads were operating in Canada. Some — the Wabash for example — made do with running rights over Canadian roads, but most constructed their own trackage north of the border. No U.S. road maintained a greater presence in Canada than James J. Hill's Great Northern Railway.

From his headquarters in St. Paul, Minnesota, former-Canadian Jim Hill — no doubt

A handsome but lightweight PGE 2–8–2 pauses at Squamish, B.C. in May 1949. *Paterson George Collection*

Left: Trailing a train of hoppers loaded with Kootenay mineral wealth, an unidentified Great Northern engine slowly crosses a 198-foot-long GN trestle near Phoenix, B.C. *Provincial Archives – British Columbia*

motivated by both his disdain for the CPR and his quest for new traffic — directed Great Northern construction of Canadian lines totalling 607.26 miles. Although Hill briefly flirted with the idea of building a GN line from Winnipeg to Vancouver, actual construction was limited to lines in Manitoba and British Columbia.

In a frontal challenge to the CPR, Hill gave Vancouver a mainline to Seattle and Portland (with a connection with the east–west mainline at Everett, Washington); flung a line across southern B.C., through Coquihalla Pass to Midway and Grand Forks; stretched branchlines from Bonner's Ferry, Idaho to Kuskonook, B.C.; from Rexford, Montana to Elks and Fernie, B.C.; bought Daniel Corbin's Nelson and Fort Sheppard; built the narrow-gauge

Kaslo & Sloan and even invaded Vancouver Island with construction of the 16-mile Victoria and Sydney.

In Manitoba, Great Northern's Brandon Saskatchewan & Hudson Bay Railway ran from St. John, North Dakota to Brandon, Manitoba. The Midland Railway of Manitoba — a jointly owned Great Northern/Northern Pacific venture — built from Walhalla, North Dakota to Morden, Manitoba, and from Neche, N.D. ran through Manitoba towns Gretna, Plum Coulee and Carman to a terminus in Portage la Prairie. The Midland also negotiated trackage rights over Canadian Northern's former Northern Pacific & Manitoba line from the U.S. boundary to Winnipeg, where the Manitoba Great Northern Railway established its own terminal facilities.

Well-groomed Great Northern 4–6–2 No. 1361 heads train #355 into New Westminster, B.C. on May 19, 1949. *Paterson-George Collection*

Top Right: A carryover from the days of the Northern Pacific and Manitoba, Northern Pacific 4–6–2 No. 2189 wheels a four-car train out of Winnipeg, Manitoba on Canadian National's former NP line to the border at Emerson, Man. *Paterson-George Collection*

Bottom Right: Photos of Rutland operations in Canada are rare. Fortunately, Philip Hastings was on hand at St. Johns, Quebec on April 15, 1950 and recorded Rutland 4–6–0 No. 77 on film as the southbound "Green Mountain Flyer" paused at the CNR station to entrain U.S. customs and immigration officers. *Philip R. Hastings*

The passion with which the Great Northern pursued the CPR cooled significantly with the death of Hill in 1916. Indeed, in later years the two roads would establish friendly connections and the CPR even granted GN trackage rights from Troup Junction (formerly Five Mile Point) into Nelson. The demise of the first GN line in Canada predated Hill's departure by several years. The already troubled three-foot gauge Kaslo and Slocan was put out of action in 1909 when fire destroyed several bridges. Ironically, the line was revived and standard-gauged several years later by the CPR. Although passenger service was discontinued in 1933, the former GN line remained in service until severely damaged by heavy rains in 1955.

The post World War I slump saw abandonment of extensive GN mileage in the Kootenays and Boundary District of B.C., as well as the remote Victoria & Sydney. In 1928, the GN vacated the Midland line from Gretna to Portage la Prairie. The trackage between Gretna and Plum Coulee and from Carman to Portage la Prairie was abandoned while the 25-mile segment from Plum Coulee to Carman was sold to the CPR.

The GN branch to Brandon fell victim to the Depression along with several other Great Northern lines. For 30 years this branch had hosted daily-except-Sunday international passenger trains and witnessed coal trains and grain extras thundering over high timber trestles and rotary snowplows bucking head-light-high drifts. Now it was no more.

By the late 1930s the last GN trains had been OS'ed out of Brandon and Morden, Manitoba and Fernie, B.C. However, Great Northern "Limiteds" continued to call on Winnipeg and Vancouver; fragments of the Kootenay line (which had wandered back and forth across the Washington boundary) remained in use and handsome, green-jacketed, Belpaire-boilered GN Consolidations rolled regularly through Salmo and blasted up Cottonwood Pass to Troup Junction and Nelson. The surviving GN lines in British Columbia would outlive the Great Northern itself.

THE SPOKANE INTERNATIONAL

After dealing his Spokane Falls/Nelson & Fort Sheppard to the Great Northern, Daniel Corbin resurfaced with the 150-mile Spokane, Washington–Yahk, B.C. "Spokane International." Built with encouragement and financial assistance from the CPR, the SI began operations in November 1906 as the key link in a GN-competitive bridge route. Traffic between St. Paul, Minn., and Spokane, Washington, could be routed SOO line (a CPR subsidiary) to CPR connections in Manitoba or Saskatchewan, CPR to Yahk and SI to Spokane, thus by-passing Hill lines entirely.

By 1907, passengers were being enticed to ride the SOO/CP/SI route, billed as the New Scenic Short Line between the Twin Cities and Spokane. And Schenectady-built Spokane International 2–8–0s were dragging increasing tonnage on to the CP interchange tracks at Yahk, 10.5 miles north of the Idaho border.

CP cemented this relationship in 1917 by acquiring controlling interest in the line, but when SI floundered during the Depression the CPR failed to come to the rescue and a re-organized Spokane International emerged as an independent. In spite of the split, SI's vintage Schenectady Ten-Wheelers continued

to bring international varnish into Yahk. Freights rolled over the border behind Corbin's original Consolidations, as well as second-hand UP Mikes and former Delaware & Hudson, Wooten-firebox 2–8–0s.

U.S. RAILROADS IN EASTERN CANADA

Though GN's pre-abandonment 600-plus Canadian route miles and Spokane International's 1.5 miles gave the west Canada's largest and smallest U.S.-owned rail networks, the American presence was greatest in eastern Canada, where Delaware & Hudson, Michigan Central, New York Central and Pere Marquette had built and/or bought their way into the country, and where trackage rights and pool agreements made Boston & Maine, Rutland and Wabash trains an everyday sight.

Boston & Maine, Delaware & Hudson, New York Central and Rutland all carded daily passenger trains in and out of Montreal. Every day New York Central drags and Delaware & Hudson freights tramped upgrade from the CPR's St. Lawrence River bridge at Lachine to CP yards in Montreal. Ottawa — the nation's capital — was at the end of a New York Central branchline from upstate New York. Even the Maine Central got into the act, leasing the 54-mile Hereford Railway, from the border town of Beecher Falls, Vermont, to Lime Ridge, Quebec.

THE RASPBERRY BRANCH

Maine Central's Canadian operations commenced in 1890 with the lease of Hereford Railway, affectionately known as the "Rasp-

berry Branch." For a brief season the line flourished, handling heavy lumber traffic, a daily mixed train to Beecher Falls and even rating a through passenger train to Portland. Summer meant passenger specials and summer-only Portland–Quebec sleeping-car service. Shop crews at the three-stall, wooden engine house in Lime Ridge were kept busy servicing and turning 190-class MEC passenger engines and 240-class freight engines.

Traffic on the Raspberry Branch plummeted after World War I. On October 31, 1925, the MEC discontinued all services on the branch, cancelled its lease of the Hereford Railway and retreated from Canada. In 1927, Quebec Central acquired 4.2 miles of the former MEC lines between the Quebec Central Railway junction at Dudswell Junction and Lime Ridge. Canadian Pacific picked up the line from Cookshire to Malvina, and the remainder of the Raspberry Branch was abandoned.

THE DELAWARE & HUDSON

The Delaware & Hudson had grand visions of expanding into the resource-rich regions of northern Quebec. In 1906 the company acquired the Quebec Montreal and Southern Railway — a 144-mile, Y-shaped line running from St. Lambert and from Noyan Junction (near the U.S. border) to a junction east of Sorel and along the south shore of the St. Lawrence River toward an anticipated terminus at Quebec City. The following spring, D&H added another Canadian property to its fold, the 28-mile Rouses Point, New York–St. Constant, Quebec, Napierville Junction Railway.

The Quebec, Montreal and Southern failed to meet its potential (as well as its goal of Quebec

City) and was sold to the CNR in 1929. However, possession of the Napierville Junction — linked to the D&H at Rouses Point by a 1.1-mile connecting track — was of immense benefit to the Delaware & Hudson. Although D&H trains had been running Rouses Point–Montreal via the Grand Trunk since 1875, the Napierville Junction established connections with the CPR (as well as the GTR) as Delson and brought the Delaware & Hudson one step closer to Montreal.

In 1917, D&H forsook its GTR running rights and struck an agreement with the CPR. Beginning in October, 1917, D&H passenger trains eased up to the bumper posts at CP's Windsor Station in downtown Montreal, while D&H/NJ freights worked through to CPR Outremont and/or Hochelaga yards, also in Montreal.

Under D&H control, the NJ remained a separate entity — evidenced by a handful of obviously D&H end-cupola cabooses and wide-firebox 2–8–0s with NAPIERVILLE JUNCTION stencilled on their tender-sides. For the most part, though, D&H power rolled north of Rouses Point, especially with the New York–Montreal NYC/D&H Limiteds. The Laurentian and the Montreal Limited were traditionally wheeled in and out of Montreal by elephant-eared P and P-1 class D&H Pacifics and later, by handsome Alco-built, 300-series Northerns. The NJ's own less-attractive engines were normally restricted to lesser trains.

On the platform tracks at Windsor Station and on the ready tracks at the Glen Yard roundhouse — where the CPR's Montreal passenger power was serviced — the D&H Pacifics and Northerns congregated not only

Lima-built New York Central
H6a Mikado works through
LaSalle, Quebec with an NYC
freight to CPR's Outremont Yard
in Montreal. *Philip R. Hastings*

with Canadian Pacific power, but also with engines from the Boston & Maine and New York Central. Though the Boston & Maine power was far from home — working CP–B&M pool trains between Montreal and Boston — the NYC engines (often K-11 class Pacifics) came in on locals and overnight Utica–Montreal passenger runs.

THE NEW YORK CENTRAL

New York Central's St. Lawrence & Adirondack began running trains into Montreal in 1892, exercising trackage rights over the CPR from Adirondack Junction (on the south shore of the St. Lawrence River within sight of the CPR bridge to Lachine) to Windsor Station. Adirondack Junction is a lonely outpost on CPR's mainline to St. John, New Brunswick (as well as Vermont route of the B&M pool trains). It was the northeast limit of the New York Central System, and the eastern edge of NYC's extensive Canadian trackage. Further west, a New York Central branch out of Massena, New York crossed the St. Lawrence River at Cornwall, Ontario and cut across eastern Ontario townships to Ottawa. A backwoods operation built in 1898 as the Ottawa & New York Railway, the New York Central branch

was the domain of local passenger trains and way freights until it was abandoned in 1957.

Southern Ontario was the true New York Central stronghold in Canada. The Canada Southern — opened in 1873 and leased to the Michigan Central ten years later — was the natural extension of the Water Level Route. Michigan Central quickly transformed the Canada Southern from a single-track Fort Erie–Amherstburg, Ontario bridge route (with branches from Fort Erie to Niagara-on-the-Lake and St. Clair Junction to Courtright) to a double-track speedway.

In 1883, the mainline was shortened with construction of new trackage from Essex to Windsor (relegating the Essex–Amherstburg segment of the mainline to branch line status) and from Welland to Niagara Falls. On December 20, 1883 the CASO opened the 240-foot high, double-track Niagara Cantilever Bridge spanning the Niagara River at Niagara Falls. Trackage rights over GTR's International Bridge between Fort Erie and Buffalo were retained. While most Canada Southern freights were rerouted through Niagara Falls, the majority of CASO's passenger trains took advantage of the short cut to Buffalo. The last real expansion took place in 1887, with the completion of a branch from Comber to Leamington and Sea Cliff Park on the shore of Lake Erie.

Turned out by Alco in 1927, ageing NYC Hudson No. 5202 hustles an 18-car mail-and-express train through Canfield Jct., Ontario on May 29, 1948. *Paterson-George Collection*

THE DETROIT RIVER TUNNEL

Michigan Central refinements established the Canada Southern as one of the most impressive pieces of railroad in Canada. However, one obstacle remained — the Detroit River. Shipping interests had thwarted attempts to bridge the Detroit River at Amherstburg, and early efforts to build a Windsor/Detroit tunnel were unsuccessful. While the Grand Trunk had its St. Clair tunnel in operation by 1891, the Canada Southern was forced to make do with Windsor–Detroit car ferries. With MCRR/CASO ferries averaging 1,097 cars per day by 1905, a tunnel was an unavoidable necessity.

In the spring of 1906, the Detroit River Tunnel Company, a Canada Southern subsidiary, called for bids on construction of the long-awaited international tunnel. Work got underway in October, 1906, utilizing innovative methods to overcome earlier problems with troublesome blue clay. The subterranean approaches were bored in the traditional manner, but radical techniques were employed on the underwater portion. Trenches were dredged in the riverbed along the tunnel route. Next, pre-assembled, twin-tube steel tunnel sections were sunk in the trenches and lined with concrete inside and out. The tunnel was completed on July 1, 1910, and readied for electrified train operations during the following weeks. On July 26, 1910, a two-car special, led by Detroit River Tunnel Company 7504 — one of six DRT Alco–GE steeple-cab electrics — inaugurated service through the double-track, twin-bore Detroit River Tunnel.

THE CANADA SOUTHERN

Michigan Central complemented its physical upgrading of the Canada Southern with revitalization of the railroad's locomotive fleet. New power delivered to the Canada Southern by 1910 included 33 Ten Wheelers and 46 Consolidations; for yard power, the CASO received 28 new 0–6–0s and a pair of massive 0–10–0s, specially ordered for work at Windsor. New passenger power came in the form of ten high-drivered Atlantics and 28 Pacifics. While the Canada Southern identity on these locomotives was limited to a small "C.S. Div." stencilled on their cabsides or tenders, many of the new engines were Canadian-built. Montreal Locomotive Works built most of the 2–8–0s, 0–6–0s and 0–10–0s. The CASO locomotive shops at St. Thomas built a pair of 4–6–0 Ten Wheelers in 1900 that would later gain fame as the oldest operating engines on the New York Central.

Canada Southern's autonomy was further diminished as New York Central took greater

control of the Michigan Central. CASO reporting marks appeared on fewer cars and engine tenders were emblazoned with "NEW YORK CENTRAL LINES," with only a small "M.C.R.R. C.S.Div." tucked up on the coal bunker. Gradually even this disappeared and the Canada Southern became the Canada Division of the New York Central. But for customs formalities, the international border meant little more to the NYC than division boundaries. Hudsons raced Chicago-bound passenger trains through southern Ontario's farmland, scooping water at speed from trackpans at Waterford. Mohawks slammed eastbound manifests past clapboard country depots at Comber, West Lorne, Tillsonburg and scores of other Ontario towns. Beetle-browed H-7 Mikados blasted out of Montrose, Victoria, St. Thomas and Windsor with drag freights. Ancient Ten Wheelers and Consols worked way freights on the branches to Courtright, Leamington and Amherstburg (the Niagara-on-the-Lake branch died in the 1930s). And the sprawling St. Thomas, Ontario, shops painted NEW YORK CENTRAL on the tenders of freshly shopped engines. Physically, operationally and visibly the Canada Southern was just another division on the Water Level Route.

The Canada Southern was not the only American railroad in southern Ontario. Exercising trackage rights granted by the Grand Trunk in 1898–99, Wabash dispatched mixed-freight drags and hot-shot "Redballs" from Detroit River ferry slips in Windsor to Buffalo, New York, via the former GWR Canada Air Line. On the heels on the Wabash–Grand Trunk agreement, the Pere Marquette established itself in southwestern Ontario.

PERE MARQUETTE AND THE LAKE ERIE & DETROIT RAILWAY

Pere Marquette bought its way into Canada in 1903 with the purchase of Hiram Walker's Lake Erie & Detroit Railway. The LE&D consisted of a mainline from Windsor to St. Thomas along with the former Erie & Huron Railway, a north–south, Sarnia–Erieau (on Lake Erie) line, which crossed the LE&D at Blenheim. Car ferries at Sarnia–Port Huron and Windsor–Detroit linked Pere Marquette's Canadian Division to home rails. Lake Erie boats brought heavy traffic, especially coal, to Pere Marquette slips at Erieau. Like the Canada Southern, the LE&D constructed locomotive shops at St. Thomas, though Walker's road built on a smaller scale.

Pere Marquette's motive in acquiring the isolated, dead-end LE&D became obvious in 1904, when PM signed a deal for CASO trackage rights between St. Thomas and Niagara Falls/Fort Erie. Within a year of its Ontario acquisition, Pere Marquette was hustling Detroit–Buffalo bridge traffic across Canadian soil.

Lacking a true physical connection with the rest of the Pere Marquette, the Canadian Division operated with some independence. The St. Thomas shops were kept busy maintaining Pere Marquette's Canadian-based fleet, which was dominated chiefly by American-built Consolidations and 2–8–2s. The Canadian Division conducted respectable business, with coal from the docks at Erieau and lucrative traffic from the chemical valley at Sarnia, as well as Michigan–New York transit trade. In 1947, Pere Marquette was acquired by the Chesapeake & Ohio Railroad and the Canadian Division was transferred intact to the new owner.

THE TORONTO, HAMILTON & BUFFALO RAILWAY

Though its name only hinted at the prospect, southern Ontario had yet another American railroad, albeit one with fractional Canadian ownership. Envisioned as an independent railroad linking its namesake cities, the Toronto, Hamilton and Buffalo became instead a short Hamilton–Welland bridge route (with several branchlines) controlled by Vanderbilt interests and the CPR. Vanderbilt's 73 percent stake in the TH&B was divided among NYC (37 percent), Michigan Central (18 percent) and Canada Southern (18 percent) while CPR held the remaining 27 percent.

Before even a rail was laid, the TH&B deviated from its intentions. In 1883, it bought the Brantford, Waterloo & Lake Erie — a Brantford–Waterford line in the process of extending itself from Brantford to Hamilton. The BW&LE opened in 1889, operating Brantford–Waterford trains behind its sole engine (ex-Toldeo, Canada Southern & Detroit/Michigan Central No. 314), a Grant-built 4–4–0 appropriately numbered BW&LE 1. The first Hamilton to Waterford train operated on May 24, 1895, behind TH&B's first engine — formerly BW&LE No. 2 — another ex-Michigan Central 4–4–0. Formerly Canada Southern/Michigan Central No. 318 — built by Grant in 1876 — BW&LE No. 2 became TH&B No. 12 and was scrapped at Hamilton in 1900.

The TH&B trimmed its Toronto–Hamilton–Buffalo ambitions to construction of a mainline from Hamilton to a connection with the Canada Southern at Welland. This goal was accomplished in December, 1895 and express trains to Buffalo were being advertised by 1896. The Grand Trunk granted Toronto–Hamilton trackage rights to the CPR in April 1896; a TH&B–GTR connection between Hamilton and Hamilton Junction was completed and on May 30 1896, through CP–TH&B–CASO/MCRR Toronto–Hamilton–Buffalo service was inaugurated. (In that same year, the TH&B purchased freight-only

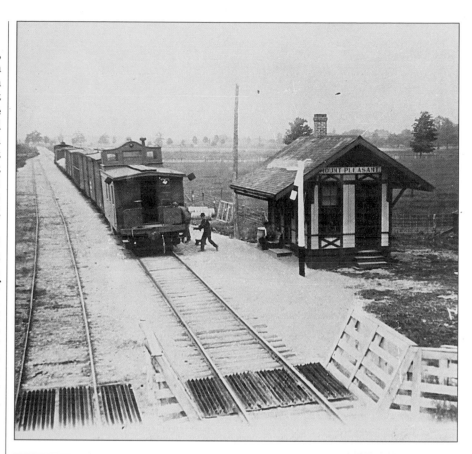

Patterned after Boston & Albany 2–8–4's, a pair of MLW-built Berkshires delivered in 1928 were TH&B's only taste of "super power" steam. Bell on the upswing, TH&B No. 201, the elder of Canada's only two native Berkshires, sprints for Hamilton with a westbound freight in the spring of 1953. TH&B GP7's were abuilding and within months, the 201 would be dead. *Paterson-George Collection*

running rights between Hamilton and Dundas over the railroad of the same name.) In a roundabout way, the TH&B had realized its goal.

Between 1896 and 1897, the Michigan Central operated the TH&B on behalf of the four owners. However, the arrangement proved unsatisfactory and the railroad reverted to home rule. Just the same, the policies determined by the road's Hamilton headquarters were heavily influenced by input from the Michigan Central and its minority partner, the CPR.

The little Vanderbilt–Van Horne stepchild enjoyed healthy business — especially bridge traffic exchanged between its parent roads. By the early 1900s, TH&B's aging fleet of 0–4–0s, Moguls and Ten Wheelers (including Baldwin 2–6–0s — built for AT&SF, but refused — and secondhand 0–4–0s from Chicago's Union Stock Yards) was in dire need of re-enforcements. New Ten Wheelers began arriving from Montreal and Schenectady in 1904, the same year that MLW delivered 0–6–0 No. 40 (first), TH&B's first six-coupled switcher. Between 1907 and 1913, TH&B received another five 4–6–0s and six more 0–6–0s. In deference to growing tonnage as well as to the 1.04 percent Hamilton–Vinemount climb up the Niagara Escarpment, MLW was contracted to build seven 2–8–0s. In 1913, TH&B No. 11 — the road's first Pacific — joined Michigan Central 4–6–2s in the Toronto–Hamilton–Buffalo passenger pool.

In 1905, the Toronto–Buffalo passenger trains were re-equipped with attractive, wood-sheathed cars built by CPR's Angus shops in Montreal. And in 1911, the TH&B gained attention as the first North American road to install Absolute Permissive Block signalling.

A brief period of expansion saw TH&B branch-lines extended from Welland to Port Colborne and from Smithville to Dunnville and Port Maitland.

From Port Maitland the TH&B launched Lake Erie car ferry service. Registered in Ohio to the Toronto Hamilton and Buffalo Navigation Company, the S.S. *Maitland* No. 1, a four-track, 32-car-capacity car ferry began Port Maitland–Ashtabula, Ohio sailings in October 1916. World War I was intensifying at the time. The *Maitland*'s U.S. registry was a ploy to prevent her from being drafted by the Canadian government. The TH&B's draft-dodging ship continued to work the 91-mile Port Maitland–Ashtabula route until June 28, 1932, when the service fell victim to the Welland Canal and was discontinued. Furloughed by the TH&B Navigation Company, the *Maitland* was cut down to a barge years later and may still be in existence.

Pressured by the demands of World War I traffic increases and by the decreasing capabilities of ancient locomotives — some dating back to the construction fleet of TH&B-builder Dominion Construction — the TH&B went shopping for more power. In 1917, the Canadian Locomotive Company delivered three 0–6–0s from its Kingston works and four used locomotives arrived on the property. A trio of Baldwin 4–4–0s built in 1905–06 for the Buffalo & Susquehanna were purchased to replace TH&B 4–4–0s Nos. 3, 4 and 5 (Baldwin 1895). In Hamilton–Waterford, local service and an ex-Pennsylvania 2–8–0 became TH&B No. 60. Formerly PRR 2762, the heavy Consolidation was acquired for evaluation on the Niagara escarpment grades out of Hamilton, but was less than successful. Its TH&B career lasted less than three years. U.S. registry may have

helped the S.S. *Maitland* avoid conscription, but there was no way to protect motive power. In 1918, the wartime Canadian Railway Board diverted three of six brand-new CLC 0–6–0s from the TH&B to the Canadian Northern. Intended to be TH&B Nos. 52, 53 and 54, the engines became, instead, Canadian Northern Nos. 500–502 and later, Canadian National Nos. 7302–7304. The new arrivals allowed retirement of the oldest TH&B power, including the last survivors of the engines inherited from Dominion construction. As old or older than the TH&B itself, a number of the veteran engines went on to post-retirement careers. TH&B No. 20, a Schenectady 4–6–0 built in 1894, went to a sugar plantation in Cuba. All three of the Baldwin Moguls refused by Santa Fe in 1894 were resold after lengthy TH&B service. Th&B No. 22 went to the St. Lawrence Railroad, No. 23 to the Arcade and Attica and No. 24 emigrated to Mexico.

After MLW delivered the final two TH&B Pacifics in 1923, the railroad turned its attention to bringing its road freight operations out of the drag era. The MLW 2–8–0s were fine on branch lines, but bigger, faster power was necessary for the hot, CP/TH&B/MCRR overhead traffic. In the quest for a 2–8–0 successor, the TH&B conducted trials with leased NYC H-10b 2–8–2 No. 355 during July, 1927. The massive H-10b was the apex of New York Central Mikado development, but when newly delivered Boston and Albany A-1b 2–8–4 No. 1433 arrived on the TH&B for the second round of testing, the TH&B men knew the search was over. The booster-equipped, 385,000-pound, Lima-built Berkshire could walk up the 1.04 percent to Vinemount with half of Kinnear Yard tied to her tender and could sprint across the flatlands at track speed.

The only Canadian-built Berkshires, TH&B 2–8–4s Nos. 201 and 202 were delivered from MLW in July, 1928 and were put to work on the "Starlight," the Hamilton–Fort Erie (later changed to Hamilton–Niagara Falls) TH&B/MCRR runthrough freight. Between Starlight assignments the Berkshires performed occasional passenger duties and TH&B lore is filled with accounts of their achievements. Operating men revelled in tales of Berks storming unassisted upgrade to Vinemount with up to two dozen passenger cars, of greater feats working the Starlight with record tonnage and of high-speed runs on the tangent track beyond Vinemount. Those fortunate enough to witness the 201 and 202 at work echo the enthusiasm.

The 201 and 202 were TH&B's only taste of superpower steam. Indeed, the two Berkshires were the last new steam purchased by the railroad. In 1948, TH&B made its last steam purchase, a pair of ex-NYC J1d Hudsons. Built by Alco in 1929, NYC 5311 became TH&B No. 501 and sister 5313 was rechristened TH&B No. 502.

New York Central Hudsons were no strangers to the TH&B. Since the mid-1930s, Central Hudsons were included in the Buffalo–Toronto passenger pool, along with TH&B, CP and NYC Pacifics. The 501 and 502 joined the TH&B roster late in the steam season and spent their TH&B careers in the Buffalo–Hamilton–Toronto pool, along with their former roster mates. Only slightly younger than the Berkshires, the two Hudsons were, by coincidence, the newest engines on the TH&B roster and the last TH&B steam to be retired.

Bottom: TH&B 0–6–0 No. 48 exits stall number three of the Chatham Street roundhouse in Hamilton, Ont. *Charles Begg Collection*

EXPANSION AND DEVELOPMENT

Northerns at night. Freshly-striped U2g No. 6207 faces younger sister U2h No. 6258 at Brockville, Ont. on August 23, 1958. *Jim Shaughnessy*

While the Canadian Northern and Grand Trunk Pacific/National Transcontinental raced to complete the nation's second and third transcontinental railroads, while the White Pass tried to tame the Arctic, and while Hill invaded the west, the Canadian Pacific — the continent's first transcontinental railroad and self-proclaimed as the "World's Greatest Travel System" settled down to the business of running a railroad. CPR began refining its operations, upgrading its physical plant and improving the tools of its trade. For the CPR, development was the new frontier.

THE ANGUS SHOPS

Company shops took an active role in the development of new technology and equipment — notably locomotives. The first CPR-built locomotive, a diminutive 4–4–0 numbered 285, rolled out of the company's Delormier Avenue shops in the east end of Montreal in 1884. By the turn of the century, the CPR had outgrown the Delormier shops. In 1904 the company opened the Angus shops, a sprawling east-end Montreal complex spread over 37 acres.

Angus was more than just a railroad shop. It was one of Canada's premier industrial facilities. Foundries, machine and carpentry shops, blacksmith shops, steel-casting, pattern, brass and tinsmith shops, one of the largest lumber-planning mills in Canada, as well as a power plant, heating plant, hospital, ambulance service and even a firehall were all located within Angus's 4,800-foot-by-2,100-foot perimeters. Angus was as self-sufficient as possible. The wheel foundries were capable of producing more than 90,000 locomotive and car wheels per year. There were truck shops, tender shops, passenger-car shops, electric shops, and upholstery shops. Car shops were capable of about 100 repair jobs a day. The locomotive shops could perform class repairs on more than a dozen engines at one time. At peak capacity, Angus could build five new steam locomotives, ten passenger cars and 40 freight cars per month.

In November 1904, CPR 0–6–0 No. 2045 rolled off the erecting floor at Angus. In the next 40 years, 677 more Angus-built locomotives would emerge from the Montreal shops. Though its capabilities were overwhelming, Angus could not singlehandedly satisfy the CPR's voracious appetite for new and reconditioned locomotives and rolling stock. The company's major shops at Winnipeg (Weston shops, opened in 1907) and Calgary (Ogden shops, completed in 1913) were also kept busy. In addition, the erecting halls of the country's two major locomotive builders — the Montreal Locomotive Works and the Canadian Locomotive Company (Kingston, Ontario) — were frequently crowded with new CPR engines. And the order books of domestic car builders were traditionally filled with Canadian Pacific contracts.

CPR POWER

Although the CPR was an early advocate of eight-coupled and ten-coupled power (the railroad had 2–8–0s at work in the mountains soon after it opened, and rostered Angus-built 0–10–0s and 2–10–2s by World War I), the road's motive-power policies favoured smaller engines. Ten Wheelers were staple power on the CPR. The company rostered its first 4–6–0 in 1889 and amassed a fleet of nearly 1,000 (including 503 D10s — the most numerous single class in Canada) by the time the last one was completed in 1915. Consolidations were drag freight contemporaries of the dual service 4–6–0s until Pacifics and Mikes bumped the veterans into secondary service. In the mountains, Decapods that arrived on the scene during World War I were supplemented by 2–10–2s and ultimately by massive 2 10 4 Selkirks.

Except for six 0–6–6–0s built by Angus for service on Field Hill, Canadian Pacific — indeed all Canadian railroads — eschewed articulated power. In fact, after a few short years in British Columbia, CP's half dozen 0–6–6–0s (outshopped between 1909 and 1911) were returned to Angus, re-emerging from

Top : Nearly 30 engines in various stages of overhaul crowd the erecting hall of Angus Shops in Montreal in this 1930 view. *Public Archives Canada*

Top Centre: Baldwin-built, CPR class L5a 2–8–0 No. 3165 stands in front of the Kamloops, B.C. station in an undated photo taken during the 1920s. *Canadian Pacific Collection*

1910–17 as R2 class 2–10–0s Nos. 5750–5755.

While other roads equated bigger with better power, CP chose to refine existing types, experimenting with compounds (between 1891 and 1911, CP operated over 360 compounds, including 4–4–2s, 4–6–0s, 2–8–0s and the first five 0–6–6–0s) and pioneering in superheating — there were 350 superheated engines on the property by 1907. By World War I, Pacifics and 2–8–2s were the order of the day.

Canadian Pacific's endorsement of medium-sized power was not the result of blind prejudice. The railroad sampled a pair of Angus-built 4–8–4s in 1914 and commissioned Angus to construct two 4–8–4s in 1928. After evaluations CP ruled out further 4–8–2s. The company elected not to participate in the continent-wide trend toward dual-service Northerns. Instead it standardized with legions of 4–6–2s and 2–8–2s, 65 dual-service Hudsons, a fleet of light (and very fast) 4–4–4 "Jubilees" — and for the Rockies, standard and semi-streamlined Selkirk 2–10–4s.

CP embraced the Pacific with almost as much enthusiasm as it had afforded its predecessor the 4–6–0. A total of 498 4–6–2s accumulated on the CPR roster between the arrival of the company's first Pacific — G2a No. 1150, turned out of Angus in January, 1906 — and the August, 1948 delivery of the last one — CLC-built G5d No. 1301. Maids of all work, CPR Pacifics built at Angus, MLW and CLC came in classes G1 through G5, with a multitude of subclasses. They came in lighter versions, classed G1, G2 and G5 and as heavy-weight G3 and G4s. They were utilitarian beasts. Later G3s were afforded sunken headlights and skirted running boards in a poor-man's version of H. B. Bowen's classic Jubilee/

Royal Hudson/Selkirk streamlining. CPR Pacifics were at home system-wide, heading passenger trains from the maritimes to the Pacific coast; working grain extras across the Saskatchewan prairie; labouring out of Toronto with manifests and rolling commuters and Limiteds in and out of Montreal. They worked on and were lettered for subsidiaries Quebec Central and Dominion Atlantic; they were leased to the Northern Alberta and traditionally worked into Buffalo, New York, in the CP/TH&B/NYC passenger pool. Nearly every significant CPR terminal had Pacifics assigned to it. Roundhouse foremen could assign 4–6–2s indiscriminately to varnish and tonnage alike.

be found over most of the system. Though hauling tonnage was their forte, CPR Mikes did draw passenger assignments, especially in British Columbia. Here P1s were a familiar sight on Kootenay Division varnish; triple-headed P2s could be found lugging 15-car passenger trains upgrade through Kicking Horse Pass and semi-streamlined 5400s locked knuckles with Selkirks and Decapods to move heavyweight, solid-tuscan passenger consists through the Rockies.

THE HUDSONS

The transition from Pacific to Hudson was more evolution than revolution. When Montreal Locomotive Works delivered CPR's first Hudsons during the last two months of 1929, the H1a 4–6–4s numbered 2800–2809 revealed a combination of G3d characteristics blended with mechanical features introduced on the relatively new 2–10–4s and Angus-built 4–8–4s Nos. 3100 and 3101. The G3ds and H1as shared 75-inch drivers, Walschaerts valve gear, nearly identical maximum tractive effort statistics and weight-on-drivers within a half-ton of each other. The Hudsons, however, featured single-piece Commonwealth frames, extensive use of weight-saving nickel-steel alloys, higher boiler pressure and greater boiler capacity.

The Hudsons excelled in long-distance passenger service and were instrumental in reducing from 14 to five the required engine changes between Fort William and Vancouver. The operating efficiencies of the new engines prompted the purchase of another ten MLW 4–6–4s in 1930. Speed was another Hudson

Top: Ten-Wheelers could — and did — work every part of the CPR, from the Dominion Atlantic to the Esquimalt & Nanaimo. Here on November 4, 1953, DAR 4–6–0 No. 44 works the docks at Digby, Nova Scotia, in the company of Pacific No. 2617 and CP Bay of Fundy steamship *Princess Helene. Philip R. Hastings*

Bottom Centre: One of 503 CPR D10 class 4–6–0's, D10e No. 832 blasts upgrade to Orr's Lake, Ont., assisting Mikado No. 5135 with a westbound extra on March 9, 1957. *Jim Shaughnessy*

The all-purpose Pacifics complemented the similar-size Mikados built specifically for freight work. Indeed, the two types were often designed simultaneously and shared similar traits. Such cooperative development resulted in the G3–style semi-streamlining of the last 69 P2 class 2–8–2s built between 1940 and 1948.

The first Canadian Pacific 2–8–2, P1a No. 5000 (later rebuilt and numbered 5100) rolled out of Angus in August, 1912. During the next 36 years Angus (whose Mikado production would include engines rebuilt from 2–8–0s), MLW and CLC would supply the CPR with 333 more Mikes. Like the Pacifics, the 2–8–2s could

asset. The overnight Toronto–Montreal passengers — No. 22, the "Overseas" and No. 21, the "Chicago Express" (whose heavyweight consists frequently swelled to more than 18 cars) were the domain of the company's two K-1 4–8–4s Nos. 3100–3101. CPR 2800s handled the accelerated schedules of Nos. 19 and 38, the regular afternoon Montreal–Toronto/Toronto–Montreal trains. Introduction of the H1s on these trains prompted schedule reductions and for a brief period in 1931, No. 38, the "Royal York" held the record as the fastest scheduled train in the world with

a 6 hour 15 minute Toronto–Montreal dash. The CPR Hudsons were capable of exceeding 100 mph and frequently beat the record

While the Depression put Canadian Pacific's Hudson programme on hold, the mid-1930s passion for speed, streamlining and light-weight equipment spawned a group of fleet-footed, 80-inch drivered, semi-streamlined 4–4–4s. Developed under the direction of CPR's Chief of Motive Power, H. B. Bowen, the first five "Jubilees" F2a class 4–4–4s Nos. 3000–3004 were built by MLW in 1936. Four of the five engines were assigned to Montreal–

Quebec City trains, while No. 3001 went west to work the Calgary–Edmonton "Chinook."

Heavy-handed hoggers racked up impressive, but unofficial, speed records with lightning-fast 3000s. Not surprisingly, a Jubilee F2a 3003 clocked at 112.5 mph near St. Telesphore, Quebec, on the Winchester Sub. on September 18, 1936, held the official Canadian speed title for 30 years. The circumstances of the run are unusual. The speed was documented, not in an attempt to clock the Jubilee, but rather on an airbrake test train sponsored by the brake manufacturer, Westinghouse.

In the fall of 1937, CP began taking delivery of the first of 20 CLC-built F1a Jubilees. Numbered 2910–2929, the CLC 4–4–4s had been designed to make them suitable, not only for fast mainline running, but for secondary branchline service. The F1s rode on smaller (75-inch vs. 80-inch) drivers, had smaller cylinders and weighed in 36,500 pounds lighter than an F2 in working order. They had a slightly lower tractive effort, shorter wheel base, smaller fire box and measured five feet shorter than an F2. The most notable difference, though, was the modified front end of the F1a. Gone was the shroud that enclosed the F2s front end from coupler to cylinder and from pilot to smoke box. Instead, the CLCs sported solid pilots, exposed cylinders and an even cleaner smoke box front than the F2a — in short, one of the plainest faces in railroading. It was, however, a face that had been seen before. Two months before, in fact, for Bowen had applied the simplified Jubilee semi-streamlining to the newest order of Hudsons. In September, 1937 MLW had begun turning out H1c 4–6–4s in the dress that would grace a total of 45 Hudsons, as well as 16 2–10–4 Selkirks. It was a classic design, featuring solid pilots, moon-faced smoke boxes with recessed headlights, shrouded exhaust stacks, skirted running boards, domeless boilertops and smooth-lined all-weather cabs — an inimitable look that would be forever synonymous with Canadian Pacific steam, even though it was worn by only a fraction of the more than 3200 steam locomotives in the company's history.

Bottom Left: Bound for Slocan City and Roseberry, B.C. on May 21, 1951, CPR M4g class 2–8–0 No. 3480 rushes mixed train #M–841 along the Kootenay River at Taghum, B.C. *Philip R. Hastings*

Top Left: The morning line-up at Nelson, B.C. on May 21, 1951 included N2a 2–8–0 No. 3677, P1n 2–8–2 No. 5261 and R3b 2–10–0 No. 5758. *Philip R. Hastings*

Top: Between 1909 and 1911, Angus outshopped a half-dozen 0–6–6–0's for use on Field Hill. Canada's only articulated road power, CPR Nos. 1950–1955 were sent back to Angus during World War I and re-emerged as R2 class 2–10–0's Nos. 5750–5755. *Canadian Pacific Collection*

Centre: While they may have been short-lived as 0–6–6–0's, CPR Nos. 5750–5755 enjoyed notable longevity after conversion to 2–10–0's. Eventually bumped into heavy yard and transfer duty, all six R2's lasted to the end of the steam era. One-time 0–6–6–0 No. 5752 is shown at Montreal, Que. in the late 1950s. *Jim Shaughnessy*

Beneath their stylish dress, the 30 H1c Hudsons (Nos. 2820–2849) purchased from MLW in 1937 were the same machines as their conventionally dressed predecessors. MLW delivered another ten highly rated, semi-streamlined H1s in 1938. The achievements of No. 2850 — the first of the 1938-built H1ds — would bestow a permanent honor upon all semi-streamlined Canadian Pacific Hudsons.

During the 1939 Royal Tour of King George VI and Queen Elizabeth, the 2850 was chosen to power the royal train while on Canadian Pacific rails. The westbound Quebec City–Vancouver, B.C. portion was routed over the CPR for all but the Ottawa–Brighton, Ont. segment, which was handled by CN. The 2850 was specially outfitted for the occasion and worked coast to coast, resplendent in an attractive blue and silver dress — highlighted by a stainless-steel boiler jacket, cast-metal replicas of the royal coat of arms above the headlight and on the tender sides and sporting small cast replicas of the royal crown on the running board skirts above the cylinders. The 2850 performed flawlessly, handling the 3,224-mile, transcontinental journey without relief. Sister No. 2851 — wearing standard CPR tuscan and black dress — accomplished a similar feat, assigned to the pilot train on the same tour.

Following the visit, designer Bowen sought — and received — royal assent to place em-

bossed crowns, similar to those worn by the 2850 during the tour, on the skirts of all of his semi-streamlined Hudsons. As the crowns were affixed to their skirted running boards — above and just ahead of the cylinders — the H1s, whose elegant dress had been borrowed from a spirited class of Jubilees, were christened "Royal Hudsons."

Canadian Pacific's final Hudson order — for five oil-burning H1es, to be assigned to the Vancouver–Revelstoke, B.C. passenger pool — was completed by MLW during the war-torn month of June, 1940. Born into royalty, H1es 2860–2864 arrived on the property with crowns firmly in place — the last Royal Hudsons.

THE SELKIRKS

The ultimate application of Bowen's so-called "semi-streamlining" was the adaptation of the Royal Hudson styling to suit two classes of 2–10–4 Selkirks, built for service between Calgary and Revelstoke. The first examples, T1bs 5920–5929 rolled out of MLW during 1938, while the final six, T1cs 5930–5935 were delivered in 1949, when the curtain was already closing on steam operations.

Streamlining engines that were designed

and built to slug it out in grueling mountain mainline work was an unorthodox move, but the massive Selkirks wore it well. Their classic Royal Hudson lines complemented by a modified version of the T1a's distinctive inward-sloping cab sides, the new Selkirks were deceptively dapper. Beneath all the moon-faced, smooth-lined, skirted styling was a brute of a machine that — ready to roll — tipped the scales at 731,000 pounds. The Selkirks could handle passenger and freight assignments with equal ability, dragging 1,025 tons up Field Hill (where the most powerful CPR Mikados were limited to 725 tons apiece and where even 2–10–2s were good for no more than 825 tons) and, if set loose on the prairies east of Calgary — as they regularly were by the early 1950s — could handle a 5,000-ton freight with ease.

Unfortunately, the last six Selkirks, built by MLW in 1949, were born too late. Accepted from MLW in March 1949, T1c 5935 was the last steam locomotive purchased by the CPR. Diesels were closing in, and by the summer of 1957, No. 5935 and her still-young sisters were on the dead-lines behind Calgary's Ogden Shops.

Centre: **Contrary to popular belief, the prairies are not entirely flat and, in fact, have several areas that required helper service in the steam age. On one of CP's steepest "flatland" grades, Decapod No. 5782 assists G3 Pacific No. 2349 and train #978 out of the Assiniboine River valley at Minnedosa, Manitoba on April 19, 1953. *Paterson-George Collection***

Top Left: **In more familiar Decapod country, R3 2–10–0 No. 5773 doubleheads with a T1 class 2–10–4 on an eastbound express train in the Lower Canyon of the Kicking Horse River, B.C. *Canadian Pacific Collection***

Bottom: **Forty-three-year-old Quebec Central G2s No. 2536 and less-than-ten-year-old CPR P2j Mikado No. 5449 doublehead an eastbound extra through Johnville, Quebec on January 29, 1954. *Jim Shaughnessy***

Left: **Outshopped in the year following the Intercolonial Railway's acquisition of Canada's first 4–6–2, 1906-vintage CPR G1r Pacific No. 2203 helps 2–8–2 No. 5187 uphill through Campbelleville, Ont. on August 1, 1954. *Jim Shaughnessy***

LOCOMOTIVES OF THE CN

In contrast to the CPR, where a stable corporate and financial situation allowed the locomotive roster to evolve naturally with the growth and needs of the railroad, Canadian National motive power managers were thrust into the position of systemizing the combined and complex rosters of the Canadian Northern, the Canadian Government Railways, Grand Trunk and Grand Trunk Pacific. The engines inherited by the Canadian National between 1919 and 1923 ranged from ancient GTR 4–4–0s to modern, vestibule-cabbed CGR 2–10–2s.

The amalgamation of the Canadian Northern and Canadian Government Railways in 1919 produced a manageable, almost orderly fleet. Canadian Northern's Hungerford administration had cleaned house in years before the takeover, ridding the railroad of most of its older, infirm power. Thus, the 797-engine CNoR roster of 1919 — while lacking larger power — was dominated by a capable fleet of 4–6–0s, 2–8–0s and 0–6–0s, many of which lasted until the 1950s.

Minus the 27 narrow-gauge engines assigned to PEI, the Canadian Government Railways' 772-engine standard-gauge roster (801 including PEI) was just slightly smaller, but custom-tailored to fill the voids in the Canadian Northern fleet. Like the Canadian Northern, the CGR owned few engines smaller than a Ten Wheeler and Consolidations were a common denominator (CNoR 290/CGR 238). However, where the CNoR had specialized in 4–6–0s, the government railway had opted for larger power, including Canada's first Pacifics and 2–10–2s. Canadian Northern's sole 2–8–2 was joined by 190 CGR Mikes. While CanNor rostered only four Pacifics, the CGR fleet checked in at 122. For yard power, the two roads shared a preference for 0–6–0s; eight-coupled switchers numbered less than ten, although CGR was in the process of converting 2–8–0s into 0–8–0s when the railroads were merged. CGR's 20 2–10–2s (including Canada's first — CGR No. 2000, Alco No. 1916) became Canadian National Nos. 4000–4019, and like most of the new CGR engines, remained in service until the end of CNR steam.

In sheer numbers, Grand Trunk/Grand Trunk Pacific made the largest contribution to the Canadian National roster. However, ancient 4–4–0s and 2–6–0s — some of which were out of service and most of which would not last beyond the 1930s — weighed heavily in the 1,576-engine GTR/GTP total. The Grand Trunk fleet did include very significant numbers of relatively new Consolidations (256), 2–8–2s (168), Pacifics (120), 0–6–0s (242) and even a small group of 0–8–0s (27). These, together with the previously mentioned CGR

and Canadian Northern engines, would form the foundation of Canadian National's motive power fleet for decades to come.

From the 3,256 inherited locomotives and the disparate policies of its predecessors, Canadian National derived the basics of its own very distinctive motive power strategy. Practices of the predecessor railroads — from Canadian Northern-style numberplates to the enclosed cabs favored by the CGR — were adopted by the CNR, but the government road wasted little time in charting its own course in the development of new power. The hundreds of inherited Pacifics, Ten Wheelers and Consolidations all but satisfied the CNR's long-term need for medium-sized engines. Indeed, after 1923, CN purchased no road power

smaller than a 2–8–0.

Eight-coupled power loomed large in CN's future. There were 359 Mikados and 784 2–8–0s on the property after the Grand Trunk joined the system in 1923. In that same year, CN endorsed its commitment to eight-coupled power with the receipt of a number of 0–8–0 switchers, 45 new 2–8–2s and more significantly, its first 4–8–2s. Completed by the Canadian Locomotive Company's Kingston, Ont. works during the summer of 1923, CNR U1a 4–8–2s Nos. 6000–6015 were the precursors of a dual-service, eight-coupled locomotive fleet that would peak at 286 engines.

While Canadian National's U.S. subsidiaries (Grand Trunk, Grand Trunk Western, Central Vermont and Duluth Winnipeg & Pacific) were granted a nominal amount of individuality, CN kept a relatively tight rein on their motive power policies and purchases. Accordingly, the 86 engines purchased by CN in 1924 included five Pacifics, ten Mikados and 15 0–8–0s built by Alco and assigned to the GTW. The following year, GTW received five obviously CN-influenced 4–8–2s from Baldwin.

The balance of CN's 1924 purchase was filled out by 30 2–8–2s, another 21 CLC 4–8–2s and five 2–10–2s. Built by CLC for heavy transfer and helper service in Toronto, T2a class 2–10–2s Nos. 4100–4104 weighed in at 327 tons apiece (engine and tender) and laid claim to the title of largest locomotives in the British Empire. The fat-boilered, low-drivered 2–10–2s wore beetle-browed overhanging Elesco feedwater heaters and featured the enclosed cabs that had become characteristic of heavy CNR road power. In addition, they were the first CN engines to trail the 12-wheel, cylindrical Vanderbilt tenders that would soon become a CNR standard.

THE NORTHERNS

In June 1927, the logical successor to the CN 6000 series 4–8–2 Mountains, and heir to the dual-service crown emerged from the Kingston, Ont. plant of the Canadian Locomotive Company. Her brow furrowed by an overhanging Elesco feedwater heater, cab enclosed in deference to cruel Canadian winters and tender, a 12-wheel Vanderbilt, U2a 4–8–4 No.

6100 possessed the classic CNR lines. Seventy-three–inch drivers that could dig in and roll an 80-car time-freight or race across two or more divisions with a 16-car passenger train, and an axle-loading that would permit use on secondary mainlines that were the domain of Pacifics and Mikados, defined the Northern Type as the quintessential dual-service locomotive for the CNR. These engines were forerunners of a fleet that would eventually total 203. Fifty-two 4–8–4s were placed in service on CN lines in 1927: CLC and MLW split production of 40 CNR 6100s and Alco supplied subsidiary GTW with 12 similar engines numbered 6300–6311.

With the success of the 4–8–4s, Canadian

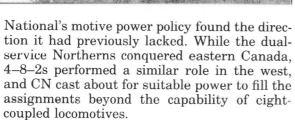

National's motive power policy found the direction it had previously lacked. While the dual-service Northerns conquered eastern Canada, 4–8–2s performed a similar role in the west, and CN cast about for suitable power to fill the assignments beyond the capability of eight-coupled locomotives.

A shortage of heavy freight power was answered with the 1928 purchase of ten ex-Boston & Albany 2–10–2s and the arrival of 33 CLC-built 2–10–2s during 1929 and 1930. The only 2–10–4s in the CN family arrived in late 1928, in the form of Alco-built Central Vermont "Texas" types Nos. 700–709.

Intense, high-speed competition for the Montreal–Toronto passenger trade prompted the purchase of five 80-inch drivered Hudsons from MLW in 1930. Classed K5a and numbered

Right: Panned at speed near Louiseville, Quebec, F2a Jubilee No. 3004 races train #357 (with a consist including two Budd RDC's and a 2200 series coach) toward Montreal on November 26, 1955. *Jim Shaughnessy*

Centre Right: Royal Hudson No. 2823 hurries through Dorval, Que., bound for Windsor Station in downtown Montreal. *Jim Shaughnessy*

Bottom: Long-time holder of the Canadian speed record, CPR Jubilee No. 3003 works Quebec City–Montreal local #349 through Lavaltrie, Que. on September 8, 1948 — 12 years less ten days after she touched a record-breaking 112.5 m.p.h. at St. Telesphore, Que. *Philip R. Hastings*

Top Right: Framed in a doorway at the Glen roundhouse, H1c Royal Hudson No. 2828 simmers away the evening of April 27, 1957. *Jim Shaughnessy*

Bottom Right: "The" Royal Hudson No. 2850 poses in full Royal Train regalia at the Glen on June 17, 1939. CPR's most famous Hudson has been preserved at the Canadian Railway Museum at Delson, Quebec. *Paterson-George Collection*

5700–5704, the handsome CN speedsters were
assigned to Montreal–Toronto service and
pitted against formidable CPR dual-service
Hudsons handling — among other trains —
No. 38, the world's fastest scheduled train in
1931.

From 1926 through 1931, Canadian National
briefly revived the tradition of company-built
locomotives. The Pointe St. Charles Shops in
Montreal — where the Grand Trunk had constructed scores of home-built engines, as large
as Pacifics and as recent as five 0–8–0s outshopped in 1923 — built 19 0–8–0s, 12 Consolidations and three 2–8–2s. Winnipeg's
former GTP/NTR Transcona Shops turned out
a dozen 2–8–0s (including N5c 2747 — the first
locomotive built in western Canada) and 21
0–8–0s, while the Moncton, New Brunswick
shops completed five 0–8–0s.

The 24 home-built Consolidations and 45
0–8–0s were the last of their type to be
acquired new by the CN. Specially designed to
cope with poor water supplies on the prairies,
PSC-built 2–8–2 No. 3800 inspired an order for
only five copies — delivered from CLC in 1936.
The season of CNR-built power — which closed
in November, 1931, with the completion of N5d
2–8–0 No. 2758 at Transcona — was an end,
rather than a beginning. On Canadian
National, the future clearly belonged to the
outside-produced, dual-service eight-coupled
locomotive.

Canadian National made considerable
efforts to refine the 4–8–4. Most of the improvements were subtle — more efficient
steam piping, roller bearings, redesigned
frames, improved riding qualities and the
change from spoked to Boxpok driving wheels.
However, in 1936, five semi-streamlined, 6400
series Northerns were delivered from MLW.
Designed (in cooperation with the National
Research Council) in an attempt to remedy the
problem of smoke obscuring visibility from the
cab, the 6400s were striking in appearance.

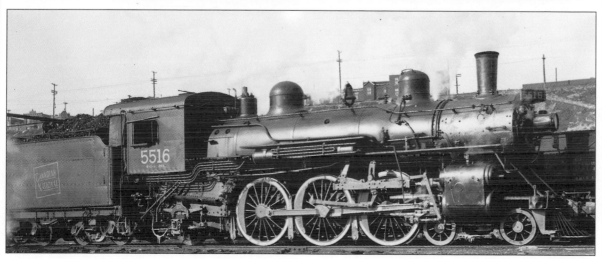

Top Left: Canadian Northern's 797-engine roster at the time of the CN takeover was dominated by a capable fleet of 4–6–0's, 2–8–0's and 0–6–0's, many of which lasted in service until the 1950s. CN N1a 2–8–0 No. 2411 — photographed at Vancouver, B.C. in 1945 — was built for Canadian Northern by Canada Foundry in 1912 and was not retired until 1959. *Paterson-George Collection*

Centre Left: With less than ten months to live, brand-new T1c Selkirk No. 5933 storms out of Banff, Alberta on May 8, 1949, with train #7. *Paterson-George Collection*

Bottom Left: Canadian National inherited a total of 414 2–6–0's from the Grand Trunk/Grand Trunk Pacific. Most, however, were ancient, pre-turn-of-the-century relics, such as CNR 593 — a home-built Mogul turned out of Pte. St. Charles in 1889 at GTR 2458. Few of these engines lasted beyond the 1930s, although the 593 — seen here at Beeton, Ont. in November 1936 — was not retired until 1943. *Paterson-George Collection*

Top : On home turf, a pair of ex-Canadian Northern 4–6–0's, led by No. 1332, push a steam-powered rotary snowplow into battle with heavy drifts on CN's Delorraine line in southern Manitoba, during the winter of 1949. *Canadian National photo*

Centre : A Baldwin graduate of 1911, CN 4–6–0 No. 1348 — seen at Palmerston, Ont. in August 1957 — was built for Canadian Northern subsidiary Duluth Winnipeg & Pacific, transferred to CN and remained active until 1959. *Jim Shaughnessy*

Left : A direct descendant of Canada's first Pacific — built for the Intercolonial Railway in 1905 — CN No. 5516 was outshopped by the same builder in 1911 and came to the CNR as Canadian Government Railways No. 443. *Paterson-George Collection*

95

Top : Freshly shopped at Winnipeg in October 1957, CNR No. 4000 — formerly Canadian Government Railways 2000 — is Canada's first 2–10–2, built by Alco's Brooks works in 1916. *Paterson-George Collection*

Right : One of 15 MLW-built Pacifics ordered by the CGR, but diverted to the Grand Trunk prior to delivery, CN No. 5293 — ex-GTR No. 1521 — takes on water at Sherbrooke, Que. before leaving for Montreal. *Jim Shaughnessy*

Centre: Undergoing overhaul at CN's former Grand Trunk Stratford, Ont. shops during December 1958, U1a 4–8–2 No. 6001 rides high above the erecting floor on the shop's 200-ton Morgan crane. Along with ex-GTP 2–8–0 No. 2721 on the shop floor, the 6001 was assigned to western Canada and had been sent east for shopping at Stratford. *Paterson-George Collection*

Bottom : Built by Montreal Locomotive Works in 1918 as CGR No. 493, elephant-eared CN 4–6–2 No. 5265 hits the CPR diamond at Lennoxville, Que. on September 2, 1948 with Portland, Maine–Montreal, Que. passenger train #17. *Philip R. Hastings*

THE
ALBUM

Posed beneath 50kV catenary, British Columbia Railway GF6C's
gather on coal trains at "Teck Loadout," on the Tumbler Ridge Branch
in July, 1984. *Dale Sanders*

Leading a four-car consist, British Columbia Railway RDC3 BC31 pops
from a tunnel north of Lillooet, B.C. on BCR #2 on September 1, 1973.
John Sutherland

Trailing eight bi-level commuter coaches and a former-F7A, power-unit/cab-car, GO Transit GP40-2L No. 702 leans into the curve at Port Union, Ont., making a dash for Toronto Union Station. *Greg McDonnell*

On the verge of being replaced themselves, CPR Baldwin DRS4-4-1000's Nos. 8000 and 8002 drift past the Lake Cowichan, B.C. water tank that once replenished the tenders of Ten-Wheelers and Consolidations that the 8000's bumped off Vancouver Island in 1949. While the 8002 has been scrapped, No. 8000 has been held for preservation by CP Rail. *Andrew J. Sutherland*

Narrow-gauge, green-and-gold Canadian National G8's Nos. 801, 800 and 804 swing into a curve on the Carbonear Branch in Newfoundland on June 22, 1967. *James A. Brown*

Above: Bound for Chicago on March 4, 1984, Amtrak F40PH No. 300 climbs the Niagara Escarpment at Dundas, Ont. "International."
Greg McDonnell

Enveloped in brake shoe smoke, the head end of a westbound CPR freight, powered by a GP9/F9B/CFB16-4/GP9 lashup, exits the west portal of the Lower Spiral Tunnel, while the tail-end of the same train — still east of the upper portal — rolls overhead. *Canadian Pacific Collection*

Straining upgrade, TH&B GP7's Nos. 72, 73
and 77 crest the Niagara Escarpment
1980. *Jim Adeney*

Wearing three CN paint schemes in sequential
order, A1A GMD1's Nos. 1032, 1018 and 1005 work a
grain pick-up through Riverhurst, Saskatchewan on
June 18, 1978. *Andrew J. Sutherland*

Maintaining a Père Marquette connection
established at the turn of the century, C&O
Canadian-built SW9 No. 5240 works the Sarnia, Ont.
"Boat Yard," *Greg McDonnell*

Built by MLW in 1918, CNR No. 5250, a former Canadian Government
Railways 4–6–2, prepares to leave Georgetown, Ont. with a
westbound local passenger train on a July evening in 1957.
L. N. Herbert

New York Central's Chicago–New York hotshot NY4 accelerates past
the Canada Southern depot at Windsor, Ont., powered by NYC RS36
No. 8033, FA2 No. 1088, RS36 No. 8036 and RS11 No. 8006. Bedraggled
FA2 No. 1088 has but three years left before being traded in on a GE
U28B, but its roadswitcher companions will last until the Conrail era.
L. N. Herbert

Canadian National's one-of-a-kind, streamlined "doodlebug" D-1 enters Georgetown, Ont. on the Beeton Subdivision, en route to Hamilton in July 1957.
L. N. Herbert

Alco cabs on borrowed time meet on the Canadian Pacific at Spicer, Ont. A brace of leased, armour-yellow UP FA's rumble past CP FA1 No. 4017 and an RS10 waiting in the siding at Spicer on May 3, 1964.
James A. Brown

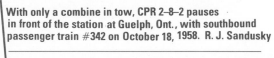
With only a combine in tow, CPR 2–8–2 pauses
in front of the station at Guelph, Ont., with southbound
passenger train #342 on October 18, 1958. R. J. Sandusky

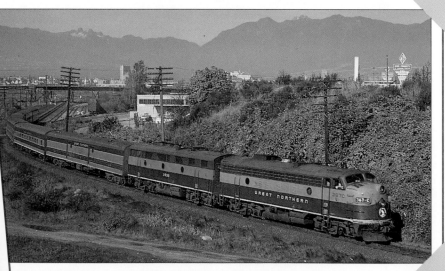

Above: The Vancouver, B.C.–Seattle, Wash. "International."
James A. Brown

Left: The Spadina Street overpass just west of CN's famed Spadina
Roundhouse in Toronto, Ont.
James A. Brown

CN Extra 9565 West
Greg McDonnell

In the pre-Agawa Canyon/Snow Train days,
Algoma Central No. 2 prepares to leave
Hawk Junction *James A. Brown*

Trailing a cloud of exhaust, coal dust and sand,
CP Rail M630's Nos. 4554 and 4560, along with SD40's
Nos. 5528 and 5527, burst from the west portal of the
Connaught Tunnel. *Charles Begg*

A blue, black, yellow and silver symbol of national unity, VIA No. 1, the "Canadian," cruises into Field, B.C. in the midst of a mountain snow storm on January 22, 1984. *F. D. Shaw*

The Detroit skyline looms on the horizon as a quartet of Canadian-built Wabash F7A's, bound for Buffalo, slam past a westbound CN passenger train at Walkerville, Ont. in October 1964. *L. N. Herbert*

Nos. 9155 and 9151 await the 18:00 departure time for VIA's "Hudson Bay" to Winnipeg — 36 hours, 45 minutes and 1,039 miles distant. *Greg McDonnell*

Ten months before it fell victim to Pepin's axe, VIA #12, the "Atlantic," skirts Bedford Basin on the home stretch of its Montreal–Halifax run on September 29, 1980. *Greg McDonnell*

A rare daylight view of the CP/TH&B/Conrail, Toronto–Buffalo, NY run-through freight "CPBU" threading through Hamilton Jct., en route to Buffalo. *Jim Adeney*

Carrying the markers and "CN" drumhead, eight-double bedroom, skyview-lounge "Malpeque" punctuates the tail-end of Jasper–Prince Rupert train #9 at Jasper, Alberta on June 25, 1971. *George Drury*

On a bitterly cold March 1984 afternoon, VIA LRC 6915 streaks along the shore of Lake Ontario at Port Union, Ont., with Toronto–Ottawa train #46. *Greg McDonnell*

Right: Two-thirds of Canada's only native E8 fleet pose together at Ottawa West, Ont. on August 3, 1962. *James A. Brown*

Above: Veteran cabs in the eleventh hour work back-to-back through McGillivray, B.C. on December 17, 1973. *Andrew J. Sutherland*

Brand-new CPR GP35's Nos. 8205 and 8204, probably on their first trip, idle at Windsor, Ont. in May 1964. *L. N. Herbert*

Near retirement, CN U2h 4–8–4 No. 6239 rests at Windsor, Ont. in March 1959, while mail is loaded aboard the baggage-express car of an eastbound passenger train. *L. N. Herbert*

Stacked three-high on CPR tri-level auto racks, brand-new General Motors automobiles glisten in the setting sun as CP Extra 5016 West hurtles through Ayr, Ont., en route to Windsor. *Greg McDonnell*

Flying white flags, Extra 2212 West passes the CN station at Pointe Claire, Que. with a pair of green-and-gold CLC H16-44's on July 9, 1962. *James A. Brown*

Running "elephant style" through spectacular scenery at Fraser, B.C., White Pass & Yukon GE "shovel-noses" Nos. 98 and 94 work toward Skagway, Alaska on June 8, 1980. *John Sutherland*

Former Erie Lackawanna C425 No. 801 (ex-EL 2451) leads BCR M420
No. 643, C425 No. 807 (ex-EL 2457) and RS3 No. 559 (ex-Lake Superior
& Ishpeming 1605) upgrade toward Fort St. John on May 21, 1981.

Wearing one of Canada's most handsome — albeit endangered —
paint schemes, five Northern Alberta Railways roadswitchers (three
GP9's and two GMD1's) stride into Clairmont, Alberta at 20:15, May 1,
1980. Nine months later, all five units will be renumbered by their
new master — Canadian National. One by one, they will lost not only
their attractive NAR dress, but their individual names, *F. D. Shaw*

Left: The former Grand Trunk station at Kitchener, Ontario briefly hosts a westbound local headed by CLC-built 4–8–2 No. 6021 on the morning of February 22, 1959. *Jim Shaughnessy*

Bottom : One of 242 ex-Grand Trunk 0–6–0's acquired by Canadian National, 09a No. 7157 — a Baldwin product of 1908 — began life as GTR No. 1708, became CNR No. 7157, then 7240 and finally 7312. After retirement in 1959, the 7312 was sold to the Strasburg Railroad in Pennsylvania, where it survives as No. 31. *Paterson-George Collection*

Right: Fresh from an overhaul at Stratford, CN's third 4–8–4 rolls extra 6102 west through Long Branch, Ont., en route to Sarnia on September 14, 1957. *Paterson-George Collection*

Centre: Two months away from retirement, CNR 2–10–2 No. 4207, ex-Boston & Albany No. 1107, lumbers past the station at "Bridge," Quebec (on the north end of the Quebec Bridge) in September 1957. *Jim Shaughnessy*

Bottom: Bilingual wig-wag signal guards a crossing east of St. Lambert, Que. as CNR Northern No. 6155 accelerates an eastbound extra freight toward the Maritimes. *Jim Shaughnessy*

Centre Right: One of 30 MLW-built 2–8–2's delivered to CN in 1924, freshly shopped oil-burning Mikado No. 3598 glistens in new paint at Winnipeg on October 10, 1957. *Paterson-George Collection*

Bottom Right: Central Vermont 2–10–4 No. 706 blackens the sky moving 88-car Montreal–St. Albans, Vt. train #430 out of St. Lambert, Que. on September 27, 1952. *Paterson-George Collection*

Despite the extensive research and experimentation that preceded construction, the effects of the semi-streamlining — which included clean lines, stylized cowls and shrouded boilertops — were purely cosmetic, and the design was repeated only on six GTW 6400s built by Lima in 1938.

Whatever the technical shortcomings of their styling, the 6400s were impressive-looking — a factor that made them a popular selection for special trains. The greatest claim to fame of the U4a class was the assignment of No. 6400 to the Royal Train of 1939. Unlike the CPR, CN utilized several engines for its portion of the tour (which included the eastbound transcontinental journey). The 6400 — although appropriately dressed for the occasion — handled the Royal Train for only a fraction of the CN mileage.

Exhaustive tests conducted in 1939, using U1b 4–8–2 No. 6020, resulted in further improvements incorporated in the construction of a total of 115 Northerns built between 1940 and 1944. When the last CNR 4–8–4, U2h No. 6264, rolled out of MLW in February 1944, the

Canadian National Northern had evolved from a beetle-browed, imposing creature to a clean-lined, stark-looking and refined machine.

Surprisingly, the final Northerns were not the last new CNR steam. The railroad that had purchased nothing (in steam) but 4–8–4s since 1936, reverted to 4–8–2s — a type last acquired in 1930 — for its final new steam power. In the last three months of 1944, MLW delivered 19 bullet-nosed, flange-stacked green-and-black U1f Mountains numbered 6060–6079.

Right: The diamond-shaped builder's plate on CN 0–8–0 No. 8395 (at Toronto about 1947) is not the familiar plate of the Canadian Locomotive Co., but that of Canadian National's Pointe St. Charles Shops, where the 8395 was built during 1930. *Paterson-George Collection*

Top: CNR U2g No. 6218 was just another Northern on June 10, 1957 when it and a CLC-built 4–8–2 doubleheaded train #401 out of Toronto for Stratford. However, six years later, No. 6218 would gain fame as the last steam locomotive to be overhauled at the Stratford shops and would spend 1963–1971 in fan trip service throughout the east. *Paterson-George Collection*

Right: Her distinctive face showing the effects of over 20 years of service, CNR U4a 4–8–4 No. 6400 — of 1939 Royal Train fame — brings a local passenger train into Niagara Falls, Ont. on September 22, 1956. *Jim Shaughnessy*

NEWFOUNDLAND JOINS THE SYSTEM

After 1944, CN would engage in several more transactions involving the acquisition of second-hand steam locomotives. For example, a half-dozen 0–8–0s were purchased from the Buffalo Creek Railroad in the summer of 1947. The most significant addition though, came in 1949, when Newfoundland — a stalwart British Crown Colony — finally joined in confederation with Canada. The Newfoundland Railway, the island colony's 704.3-mile, 42-inch, narrow-gauge network, came as part of the package. On March 31, 1949, the government-owned railroad became part of the Canadian National Railways.

The island railroad traced its roots to the original Newfoundland Railway Co., incorporated in 1881, to build from St. John's to Harbour Grace and from Whitebourne to Hall's Bay. The privately owned Newfoundland Railway collapsed after the completion of the line to Harbour Grace and was taken over by the Newfoundland government in 1884. Under government control, construction continued and lines were built and operated under various titles — including the Placentia Railway, Hall's Bay Railroad and (eventually) the transinsular, Newfoundland Northern & Western Railway, completed to Port-aux-Basques in 1897.

Much of the later construction work was performed by Robert G. Reid of Montreal, who, upon completion of the line to Port-aux-Basques, contracted to operate the island railway for 50 years. In 1898, the government-owned system was taken over by the Reid-Newfoundland Co. and engines and rolling stock were lettered accordingly. On June 29, 1898, the first regular cross-island train left St. John's and arrived at Port-aux-Basques, 547

miles, 27 hours and 45 minutes later.

Reid operated the island railroad with a fleet of 42-inch gauge locomotives, including a sizeable roster of 4–6–0s, 2–8–0s and 4–6–2s. The majority of these engines were built by Baldwin, but the locomotive shops at St. John's, Newfoundland built at least ten 4–6–0s and two Consolidations (with boilers supplied by Baldwin) between 1911 and 1916. During the 'teens, Reid went on a branchline-building spree, resulting in new lines to Bonavista, Bay-de-Verde, Grates Cove, Heart's Content, Trepassey and Terranceville, as well as aborted attempts to build to Fortune and to Bonne Bay. Construction of these branches put a strain on Reid's finances from which the company never recovered. In 1923, the government reclaimed the railroad and began operating it as the Newfoundland Government Railway. Three

Top : Posed at Toronto's Spadina roundhouse in 1957 are a pair of unmistakably CNR engines: semi-streamlined 4–8–4 No. 6404 and bullet-nosed Mountain No. 6079. Both engines were retired in April 1960. *Philip R. Hastings*

Left : A clean-lined, stark-looking, refined machine, No. 6258, CN's seventh-last 4–8–4, simmers away on August night at Brockville. *Jim Shaughnessy*

117

years later, the island railroad was renamed the Newfoundland Railway.

Under government direction, the Newfoundland Railway was honed to a more manageable system. Many of the Reid-built branchlines were abandoned during the 1930s and ancient engines — many dating to the 1890s — were replaced with new power, primarily 2–8–2s from Alco, MLW and from North British. The effects of this grooming were obvious in the railroad inherited by the CNR in 1949.

On April 1, 1949, Canadian National took over operation of a 704.3-mile (down from a peak of 968 route-miles) narrow-gauge network, which included the 547-mile, trans-insular mainline from St. John's to Port-aux-Basques and the following branchlines: Brigus Jct.–Carbonear, Placentia Jct. to Placentia and Argentia, Soal Harbour–Bonavista and Notre Dame Jct.–Lewisporte. The island railroad was staffed by a reasonably modern fleet of locomotives, dominated by 30 2–8–2s, the oldest of which were Alco graduates of 1930 and the newest members six out-shopped from MLW in 1949. The Newfoundland Railway even boasted a trio of diesels, three GE 47-tonners purchased in 1948 for yard service.

Despite the youth of its narrow-gauge Mikados, CN wasted little time in dieselizing its Newfoundland operations. In December 1952, the London Ontario plant of General Motors Diesel outshopped CNR NF110 No. 900, the first of a custom-designed breed of NF series, 42-inch gauge end-cab road switchers destined to kill steam in the tenth province. The 1200-hp, NF110 — and its nearly identical

successor, the NF210 — was an ungainly looking creature, a low-cut, mutant Geep with a scaled-down version of the familiar GP7/GP9 long hood, an unusual cab and skirting that camouflaged its C-C, narrow-gauge trucks.

Nevertheless, the NF110/NF210s were just what the doctor ordered. The 900 was followed by an additional eight NF110s in early 1953 and NF210s began arriving in force in the summer of 1956. While green-and-gold 900s took over the island, the transinsular passenger train, the "Caribou," remained in the hands of steam (often double-headed 300 series Mikados) until the arrival of seven steam generator cars in the latter half of 1956.

By 1957, the 35 NF110/NF210s and half-dozen export model GMD-built G8s on the island banished even the eight-year-old MLW 2–8–2s to the scrapyards. Less than a decade after Confederation, the former Newfoundland Railway was all diesel.

Amalgamation of the Temiscouata in 1950 added five ancient Ten Wheelers to the CN roster and in 1953, two MLW 0–6–0s (renumbered CN 7542–7543), acquired part-and-parcel with the National Harbours Board Railway in Vancouver, B.C., became the last steam locomotives to join the CN roster. For all intents and purposes though, CN closed the book on steam in December 1944, the day it accepted delivery of a bullet-nosed U1f 4–8–2 No. 6079 bearing MLW serial number 72776. On the railroad whose roots traced back more than a hundred years to the Champlain & St. Lawrence and a tiny 0–4–0 named *Dorchester*, steam was on the way out.

Top Left: Soon to become Canadian National Railways No. 324, 42-inch gauge Newfoundland Railway 2–8–2 No. 1024 prepares to leave St. John's with the passenger train to Port-aux-Basques, Nfld. *Canadian National photo*

Centre Left: Working home rails, former Temiscouata Railway 4–6–0 No. 10 — renumbered CNR 1018 — accelerates away from the water tank at Whitworth, Que. on April 23, 1954. The Temiscouata became part of the CNR in 1950 and the shortline's five Ten-Wheelers, Nos. 6–10, became CN Nos. 1014–1018. *Philip R. Hastings*

Bottom Left: With a red Lehigh Valley baggage car tied to her olive-green Vanderbilt tender, bullet-nosed Mountain No. 6079 — CN's last new steam locomotive — brings train #94, the New York–Toronto LV/CN "Maple Leaf," into Toronto on March 10, 1957. *Philip R. Hastings*

Top : Canadian National No. 599, an Alco-built, narrow-gauge 4–6–2 (originally NFLD No. 199) swings through an S-curve at Holyrood, Nfld. with the Carbonear mixed. *R. J. Sandusky*

Bottom : Whitecaps dot the pond at Cupid's, Newfoundland as CN #7, the Carbonear mixed train, slices the bleak Newfoundland landscape on June 21, 1956. *R. J. Sandusky*

Cape Breton coal road Sydney & Louisburg was one of the last holdouts of Canadian steam, rostering Canadian-built engines as well as hand-me-down 0–8–0's and 2–8–2's from U.S. roads such as Chicago Illinois & Midland, Cambria & Indiana, Detroit Toledo & Shore Line and Pittsburg & Lake Erie. On a September 1960 evening, second-hand S&L 0–8–0 No. 94 faces 2–8–2 No. 105 berthed in the engine house at Glace Bay, N.S. *Jim Shaughnessy*

O n a continental scale Canadian railroads were among the last steam strongholds. Indeed, Canadian Pacific was taking delivery of brand-new Selkirks when many U.S. railroads were dropping the fires on steam power as fast as builders could supply diesel replacements, and both Canadian transcontinentals continued performing class repairs and overhauls of mainline steam well past the mid-1950s. Interestingly though, both CN and CP had early exposure to diesels.

Canadian National pioneered the use of oil-electric self-propelled passenger doodlebugs with the 1925 introduction of cars 15817–15825. The year after the Canadian Locomotive Co. turned out CNR 4–8–4 No. 6100, overhead cranes in the same Kingston, Ontario erecting halls lowered 12-cylinder, 1330-hp. Beardmore diesel engines into a pair of 2–D–1 boxcabs that would become CNR Nos. 9000 and 9001.

A product of the combined efforts of Baldwin, Westinghouse, CLC and CN, the twin boxcabs — originally operated back-to-back as a married pair sharing road number 9000 — were completed in November and December, 1928 and hit the road in April, 1929. Considered inseparable, the two units (both then numbered 9000) worked a Montreal–Vancouver passenger train to demonstrate their long-distance capabilities and then settled into Montreal–Toronto passenger service.

Deemed to be among the first successful North American mainline diesels — and in fact the first large road diesels on the continent — the two units were split up in 1931 and continued to work as CNR 9000 and 9001 until withdrawn from service in the fall of 1939.

During World War II, the 9000 was drafted by the Canadian Government and sent to Transcona Shops, where it was re-engined with a 1440-hp. EMD 567 series prime mover, armour-plated and placed in service on an armoured train working on the west coast, out of Prince Rupert, B.C. The armour was removed in 1945 and CN 9000 — dramatically changed inside and out — worked in passenger service between Quebec City and Edmunston, N.B. until May, 1946. In the fall of that year, the 9000 and 9001 (which had languished in storage since 1939) were scrapped.

EARLY DIESELS

In spite of the 9000's success, CN ignored the potential of mainline dieselization and forged ahead with its steam programmes. However, a pair of yard diesels were acquired during this period: CLC outshopped Westinghouse-design visibility cab switcher No. 7700 (later renumbered 77) in May, 1929 and in 1934, GTW picked up a 1926-built, Brill boxcab originally built for the Long Island. Both of these engines were successful in their own right, but again, CN — actually one of the North American pioneers of dieselization — overlooked their significance and shelved any thoughts of large-scale diesel acquisitions. Harbingers of the not-too-distant future, CN No. 7700/77 and GTW No. 7730 (later GTW 73) laboured in anonymity and enjoyed unexpected longevity. The 77 was retired in 1962 and found its way to the Canadian Railway Museum at Delson, Quebec after a post-retirement industrial career, while GTW 73 lasted in service until 1960.

Canadian Pacific commissioned its first diesel locomotive in 1935. Bearing noticeable resemblance to Alco's high-hooded HH series switchers, CPR No. 7000 was built at National Steel Car in Hamilton, with a 550-hp. six-cylinder Harland and Wolff prime mover and English electrical equipment. The high-hooded experimental arrived on the property in November, 1937 and was assigned to the Montreal terminals. While it was not reproduced or imitated, the 7000 was an influential

Under the watchful eye of youthful caddies on the neighbouring golf course, CN No. 9000, the first large road-diesel on the continent, pauses with a five-car train at Dixie, Que., a now-abandoned station on the Montreal–Toronto mainline. *Canadian National photo*

factor in the acquisition of several Alco S2 switchers in 1943. Although few realized it at the time, this was the dawn of total dieselization.

Like most railroads at the time, Canadian roads initially dismissed internal-combustion power as fine for yard work and self-propelled passenger cars, but upheld the theory that no diesel could outperform their Royal Hudsons, Northerns and Mountains in heavy mainline service. The durability and economy of existing diesels, along with the impressive performance of demonstrator road units fielded by the builders, chipped away at steam's supremacy — especially in the U.S. — and through the late 1940s and early 1950s the steam bastions fell one by one.

Canada, by virtue of coincidental circumstance, remained a steam stronghold long after the diesel had conquered much of the U.S. The youth of literally hundreds of Pacifics, Mikes, Hudsons, Northerns and Selkirks working Canadian rails was a decided factor in the prolonged survival of steam north of the border. Age, however, was not the only criterion: into the late 1950s, Canadian Pacific kept active —

on a light-rail branch in New Brunswick — a trio of 4–4–0s as old as the company itself, and thousands of miles of prairie branchlines (especially CN) were patrolled by pre-World War I Ten Wheelers and 2–8–0s. Certainly another factor in the longevity of Canadian steam was the late start of domestic diesel production. Alco affiliate MLW did not outshop its first diesel — CPR S2 No. 7077 — until May, 1948; General Motors Diesel opened its London plant in August, 1950 and, after importing several orders of U.S.-built diesels, CLC finally began diesel production at its own plant in July, 1951.

So it was that in the early 1950s — when the tally of U.S. railroads hanging out the "all-diesel" sign seemed to increase daily — the diesel had but a toehold in Canada. However, steam's greatest strength by this time was simply in sheer numbers. Canadian diesel builders were gaining momentum and U.S.-built engines imported before the start of domestic production had established a beachhead for the invaders. There were Alco S2s and RS2s on the Ontario Northland and EMD

Top Left: Its appearance altered drastically by wartime armour-plating, the 9000 works freight west of Turcot Yard in Montreal. *Canadian National photo*

Centre Left: Remarkably, both of Canada's pioneer yard diesels have been preserved. Standing back-to-back at the Canadian Railway Museum at Delson, the elderly units afford diesel historians a unique opportunity to make first-hand comparisons of the two historically significant engines. *John Sutherland*

Bottom Left: Canadian Pacific's first diesel, high-hooded Harland & Wolff-powered No. 7000, was on the property only six months when photographed at Hochelaga Yard in Montreal on May 14, 1938. *Paterson-George Collection*

Bottom: Westinghouse-design "visibility cab" switcher CN No. 7700 emerged from CLC in May 1929 — only months after CLC outshopped CN No. 9000. While both halves of the original 9000 were eventually scrapped, the 7700 (later renumbered 77) has been preserved at the Canadian Railway Museum at Delson, Que. *Paterson-George Collection*

NW2s on the TH&B. Canadian National rostered Alco S2s, EMD NW2s, GE 70 Tonners and had two A–B–A sets of EMD F3s in through-road freight service. Canadian Pacific had assembled a fleet of Alco and Baldwin switchers and had even fully dieselized two divisions with imported power. Baldwin-built, CLC-imported DRS–4–4 1000s had banished CPR steam from Vancouver Island and a squad of Alco FAs and RS2s, along with three S2s for yard work and three EMD E8s for pooled CP/B&M passenger trains, had dieselized operations between Montreal and Wells River, Vermont.

DIESEL SWEEPS THE NATION

As the domestic builders kicked production into high gear, the diesels began to sweep the nation. Erection bays in Montreal, London and Kingston were crowded with the FAs and RSs, Geeps and Fs, C-liners and H-lines that spelled doom for Canadian steam from coast to coast.

In August, 1950, a maroon-and-cream, Toronto Hamilton & Buffalo GP7 numbered 71 emerged as the first locomotive completed by

Top : **Montreal Locomotive Works' second diesel, CPR S2 No. 7076, helps 1910-vintage D10g No. 872 uphill out of Sherbrooke, Que. with QCR train #48 on April 30, 1955. Although numbered one higher, CP S2 No. 7077 was MLW's first diesel.** *Philip R. Hastings*

Top Left: After the original No. 9000, CN's next road diesels were a half-dozen green-and-gold EMD F3's numbered 9000–9005. Nos. 9000, 9002, 9003 and 9005 were F3A's, while 9001 and 9004 were F3B's. F3A No. 9000 has been preserved in operating condition at the Alberta Pioneer Railway Association museum in Edmonton, Alberta. *Canadian National photo*

Left: Oblivious to the threat posed by MLW S2 No. 7984, CNR 0–8–0's Nos. 8226 (built by Lima in 1923, later renumbered CN 8448) and 8420 (ex-Buffalo Creek R.R. 26) work CN's Bathurst Street yard in Toronto, Ont. *David M. More Collection*

Bottom: Hudson-killers, three steam generator-equipped TH&B GP9's helped banish NYC and TH&B Hudsons from the Buffalo–Toronto passenger pool. Nicknamed "torpedo Geeps" for the "torpedo tube" air reservoirs carried atop their hoods, TH&B Nos. 401 and 403 accelerate away from the CN station at Oakville, Ont. with train #322. *Jim Walder/ David M. More Collection*

125

Canadian-built Wabash F7A No. 1160 stands at Fort Erie, Ont. with American-built CNR 2–8–2 No. 3431, an ex-Grand Trunk Baldwin, built in 1913. *Jim Shaughnessy*

Bottom: An A–B–B set of CPR F's curl the eastbound "Dominion" through the Lower Spiral Tunnel. The lead unit is just above the lower portal of the tunnel from which the train is emerging. *Canadian Pacific Collection*

Top Right: Polished and decorated for a somber occasion, Ontario Northland 4–6–2 No. 701 commemorates dieselization of "Ontario's Development Road," on a special train through Matheson, Ont. on June 25, 1957. *Paterson-George Collection*

Bottom Right: Steam swirls around three-year-old FP7A No. 1416 awaiting train #354's departure from Windsor Station in Montreal in January 1955. *Jim Shaughnessy*

the newly-opened General Motors Diesel plant in London, Ontario. Within the next few years, locomotives outshopped from the London facility would dominate the market and monopolize the rosters of entire railroads. TH&Bs purchase of seven GP7s and four SW9s killed the fires on the road's famed Berkshires and dieselized all of the line's freight operations by the summer of 1953. The delivery of three steam generator equipped GP9s sidelined the two ex-NYC Hudsons and the TH&B was all-diesel by the end of March, 1954. Algoma Central went all-diesel — indeed, all-GM — with the acquisition of 21 GP7s and two SW8s

between 1951 and 1952. Wabash dieselized its Canadian operations with a fleet of F7As, supplemented by four SW8s and a lone GP7; Chesapeake & Ohio did the same with five SW9s and 19 GP7s. Ontario Northland gave GMD the lion's share of its diesel orders, taking 22 FP7s between 1951 and 1953.

Through the 1950s, GMD's order books were bulging with contracts from CN and CP and the London-based builder was clearly the dominant force in the Canadian market. The two transcontinental giants took deliveries of almost every model in the catalogue, from SW series switchers to freight and passenger F-

units and GP9s (successor to the GP7) by the hundreds. GMD-built engines were a common sight throughout the land. Matched sets of CPR F-units curled through the spiral tunnels with manifest freights; braces of GP9s worked grain extras across the prairies; custom-built NF110/NF210 engines took Newfoundland by storm and GMD FP9s were preferred power on the premier transcontinental passenger trains inaugurated by both roads in the mid-1950s. Canadian Pacific's last cab-unit purchase was 11 FP9s and eight F9Bs ordered specifically for the Montreal/Toronto–Vancouver "Canadian." Likewise, CN ordered FP9As and F9Bs for its competing "Super Continental." However, these were CN's first GMD passenger cabs and subsequent purchases would raise the government road's FP9/F9B fleet to a total of 43As and 38Bs.

Producing locomotives manufactured from the designs of its U.S. parent — the American Locomotive Company of Schenectady, N.Y. — Montreal Locomotive Works assumed the position of Canada's number two locomotive builder in the diesel era. In the initial phase of Canadian dieselization, MLW made a strong showing with sales of S-series switchers, RS-series road switchers and FA/FB model cab and booster units. Problems with the Alco 244-series engines installed in early road units tarnished MLWs reputation somewhat, but promises of improvements and the eventual introduction of the 251 engine as a replacement brought repeat orders.

Canadian National bought the first MLW-built cab unit — FA1 No. 9400 — in April 1950 as part of an order for eight FA1s. In what would become a long-standing tradition, these and subsequent CNR MLW road units — including FA/FB2s, RS3s and RS10s, would be generally confined to lines east of Winnipeg. Canadian Pacific initially assigned FA/FB2s and RS3s to the Kootenays, but these too were

Working east of Jasper, Alberta, CN FP9 No. 6537 and an F9B lead a passenger train whose length is almost doubled by heavy head-end traffic. The 6537 was demolished in a head-on collision at Ingersoll, Ont. on August 10, 1981. *James A. Brown*

Top Centre: **Northbound for Sydney, Nova Scotia, CNR RS3's Nos. 3021 and 3009 cross the Canso Causeway, across the Strait of Canso near Port Hastings, N.S.** *Jim Shaughnessy*

Bottom Centre: **Two generations of MLW road power meet at Dorval, Que. Northern No. 6150 was outshopped from MLW in April 1929, while FA2 No. 9422 and its FB2 companion were built in 1951. The 9422 was retired in May 1966, only five and a half years after the 6150's retirement.** *Jim Shaughnessy*

transferred east after several years. Montreal-built FAs, RS3s, RS18s and dual-service RS10s and FPA/FPB2s dominated Canadian Pacific lines east of Winnipeg. Durable Alco/MLW 539-engined S-series switchers worked CPR yards from coast to coast. Although no sizeable roads went all-MLW, Pacific Great Eastern — MLW's only western stronghold — came close. The provincially owned railroad dieselized with MLW RSC3s and RS3s (after first buying GE 70 Tonners) and would remain a loyal MLW customer through the 1970s.

The Canadian Locomotive Co. faltered in the transition from steam to diesel production. CLC was the last builder to retool for diesel assembly and the Fairbanks Morse–design engines marketed by CLC were of limited appeal. With great expectations, CLC unveiled a pair of FM-design CPA16–4 "Consolidation Line" cab units on August 1, 1951. The future of the Kingston builder was pegged to the pair of C-line demos numbered 7005 and 7006, painted in CPR colours, christened *City of Kingston* and lettered Canadian Locomotive Co. Unfortunately, the C-line was no match for its competition and CLC was destined to live out its diesel-building days as the underdog.

CLC's entire production of FM-design diesels — which included freight and passenger versions of the C-line cabs, H-line switchers and road switchers and the highly touted H24–66 "Train Masters" — totalled only 206 units. MLW built more than that many 1000 hp. switchers and the CPR rostered only six fewer GP9s. While MLW diesels tended to congre-

"The First Streamlined Diesel-Electric Locomotive Built In Canada," Canadian National FA1 No. 9400 bursts through a paper banner at MLW in April 1950. Nineteen years later, the 9400 was put on display at the Museum of Science and Technology in Ottawa. *Canadian National photo*

FIRST STREAMLINED
DIESEL-ELECTRIC LOCOMOTIVE
BUILT IN CANADA

Top Centre: Train Master No. 8911, one of 21 CLC-FM H24-66's on the CPR roster, works an Extra East through Hazelridge, Manitoba in July 1957. *Paterson-George Collection*

Bottom: Crossing Ladner Creek on the now-abandoned Coquihalla Sub., CLC-built CPA16-4 No. 4057 and CPB16-4 No. 4452 lead train #12, the Vancouver, B.C.–Medicine Hat, Alta. "Kettle Valley Express," through the spectacular but forbidding Cascade Mountains that eventually defeated the railroad. *Canadian Pacific Collection*

Bottom Centre: An A-B of CNR "C-liners," CFA16-4 No. 8702 and one of only three CN CFB16-4's pass the Parsley mileboard, near Montreal in November 1955. *Jim Shaughnessy*

gate in the east, CLCs were spread out. Canadian Pacific's 89 CLCs were assigned almost exclusively to western Canada and concentrated heavily in the Kootenays; CN's 117 CLC-built engines were eastern-based, although some did time in the west when new.

THE LAST STEAM OPERATIONS

Diesels were headline news in the 1950s, but while GMD and MLW fought to gain supremacy in the Canadian market — and CLC struggled to exist on the leftovers — steam was making its last stand, from Newfoundland to British Columbia. The industry was in the midst of a revolution and those privileged enough to be on hand were witness to railroading in one of its most dramatic hours. There was a sense of urgency surrounding even the most mundane, everyday steam operations. For anything under steam, tomorrow was an uncertainty. Flue time ticked off like a countdown to execution; road failure could draw an appointment with the torch and the production schedules of London, Montreal and Kingston read like an apocalyptic timetable.

The faithful rushed to observe and record the changing of the guard. They trekked to Newfoundland, where narrow-gauge Mikados

fought in vain to keep ahead of the mutant Geeps taking over the island railroad; to Toronto, where massive 4100 series 2–10–2s — once the largest engines in the British Empire — engaged in their life-long vocation as helper engines, locking knuckles with Northerns and Mikes and back-to-back sets of F7s, FAs and CLC-built CFA16-4s to boost tonnage up Danforth Hill; to the prairies, where oil-burning Royal Hudsons continued to fulfill their dual-service role and where diesel refugees — Selkirk 2–10–4s from the west and 4–8–4s Nos. 3100–3101 among those driven from the east — worked out their final days in chain-gang freight service. On the CN, ancient, slide-valve 4–6–0s and 2–8–0s ruled the frail

Top : The faithful trekked to Newfoundland, where narrow-gauge Mikados fought in vain to keep ahead of mutant Geeps taking over the island railroad. Part of a complicated four-train meet, GMD-built "mutant Geep" NF110 No. 902 waits in the siding at Harry's Brook, Nfld. on June 19, 1956 as CN train #2 passes with double-headed MLW-built Mikados Nos. 323 and 314. *R. J. Sandusky*

Left: Rare CLC-built CPA16-5 CN No. 6704 leads an otherwise all-MLW A-B-B-A consist out of Halifax, N.S. with 18-car train #1, the "Ocean Limited." *Jim Shaughnessy*

Top: Engaging in its lifelong vocation, CNR CLC-built 2–10–2 No. 4102 assists a pair of CLC C-lines up Danforth Hill in Toronto on Oct. 21, 1952. *Paterson-George Collection*

Top Centre: On the verge of dieselization, massive T4 class CN 2–10–2's were bumped from mainline work in the mountains to secondary trains, branchlines and even Okanagan Valley passenger trains. With five more years to live, oil-burning CLC-built T4a No. 4307 leads a freight over Salmon Creek in Jasper Park, Alberta, during 1952. *Canadian National photo*

steel of prairie branches, while white-shirted designers employed by the eastern builders drafted light-footed diesel replacements. In the mountains, beetle-browed CNR T4 class 2–10–2s worked secondary mainline trains and branchlines — even Okanagan Valley passenger runs — until enough GMD GP9s could be dispatched west to kill the fires of the most stubborn holdouts.

On the verge of total dieselization, Montreal — with steam dispatched around the clock from CNR's Turcot roundhouse, CPR's St. Luc (the second-last roundhouse built in North

Left: One by one the steam bastions fell. Displacing steam in helper duty on Dundas Hill, CN GP9 No. 4459 assists CN Extra 6147 West through Hamilton West, Ont. in May 1958. Dieselization would soon eliminate the need for helpers on Dundas Hill. *Philip R. Hastings*

Centre Left: Canadian Pacific's legendary New Brunswick-based trio of 4–4–0's was completed by A2q No. 144, built by CPR in 1886 and A1e No. 29, built by CP's Delormier Avenue Shops in Montreal in 1887. All three locomotives have been preserved; No. 29 and No. 144 are at Delson, while No. 136 survives in operating condition as the property of Ontario Rail. *Philip R. Hastings*

Left: CLC's answer to the need for an all-Canadian A1A roadswitcher were the H10-64 and H12-64, of which CN bought the only examples. Most were assigned to the Maritime provinces, as was H12-64, seen on a local passenger train at Pictou, N.S. on May 21, 1960. *James A. Brown*

Bottom : Late in the steam season, CPR maintained a trio of ancient 4–4–0's in New Brunswick for use on a light-rail branchline out of Chipman. Completed by Rogers in 1883, CPR A2m class 4–4–0 No. 136 was Canada's oldest active steam locomotive when photographed live at Chipman on September 2, 1958. *Paterson-George Collection*

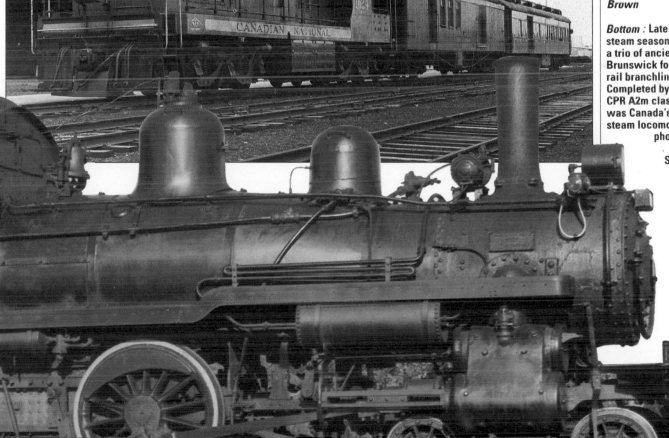

Far Left: Seemingly unaffected by dieselization, CN's ancient boxcab electrics — joined in 1950 by a trio of new GE centre-cab electrics — continued to grind in and out of Montreal under CN's north-end electrification. English Electric-built, ex-National Harbours Board boxcab No. 188 exits the south portal of the Mount Royal Tunnel with a southbound passenger train on August 25, 1956. Redevelopment has since put this scene underground, but the electrics roll on. *Jim Shaughnessy*

Left: Tiny ex-CN 0–6–0 No. 7260, a one-time Intercolonial Railway engine built by CLC in 1906, switches coal hoppers at the Drummond Colliery at Westville, N.S. on a bitterly cold January 24, 1962. Although no longer active, this engine is still in existence. *R. J. Sandusky*

Centre: General Electric 70-tonners helped dieselize CN operations on Prince Edward Island and spent most of their lives on the island railroad. Green-and-gold 70-tonner No. 39 switches the ferry slip at Borden, PEI in August 1962. *Jim Shaughnessy*

Bottom Centre: General Motors responded to the lightweight A1A with the six-axle GMD1. CN purchased 78 of the A1A lightweights and Northern Alberta picked up the remaining five units of a total production of 83. (CN also bought 18 four-axle GMD1's.) While the CLC and MLW-built A1A's have all been retired, the GMD1's survive and continue to work prairie branchlines. Descending into the Qu'appelle Valley, A1A GMD1 No. 1063 stops at Lebret, Sask., with Sturgis–Regina passenger train #66 on July 2, 1960. *R. J. Sandusky*

America) and "the Glen" — was a steam fan's Mecca. Meanwhile, Chipman, in a remote corner of New Brunswick, was a never-never land, where a legendary trio of CPR 4–4–0s — Nos. 29, 136 and 144 (all now preserved) — refused to acknowledge the arrival of the 20th century. Thanks to a number of fragile bridges, along with 65- and 73-pound rail, the branch from Chipman to Norton, N.B. was the exclusive domain of three never-say-die Americans in a season when even the 4–8–4 was an endangered species.

By the close of the decade, steam had retreated to a handful of outposts scattered about the country. Custom-designed, lightweight A1A-trucked diesels from GMD (the GMD1), MLW (the RSC13) and CLC (H10- and H12-64s) were displacing steam on the light-rail branches across the nation; RS18s and GP9s by the hundreds were bumping surviving freight and dual-service engines on to ever-lengthening scraplines and passenger work was being surrendered to cab units, all-purpose road switchers and Budd RDCs.

Province by province, division by division, diesels took complete control. During 1960, CN and CP recorded their last "official" steam-powered movements. Diesel failures and spot shortages prompted a handful of extra moves under steam, but by the end of 1960, the diesel reigned supreme.

In the post dieselization years, steam clung to life on Nova Scotia coal road Sydney & Louisburg, on a small number of industrial lines, at Saskatchewan collieries, on British Columbia logging lines and on the White Pass & Yukon, where narrow-gauge Mikes were kept on standby. However, these operations were primarily short, sporadic, or both — and all were on borrowed time.

Throughout the mid-1970's, power-short CP Rail squeezed every last
bit of life from battered RS3's, RS10's and FA's. Road-weary FA2
No. 4084, RS10 No. 8589, FA2 No. 4086 and deadheading S3 No. 6586
get #80 on the move out of Chatham, Ont. on July 6, 1974.
Greg McDonnell

ailroading rolled into the 1960s with renewed energy, buoyed by dieselization and determined to change both its methods of operation and its image. Railroad publicists found plenty to brag about throughout the decade: There were diesels and new-image paint schemes, piggyback and automated hump yards, unit trains, centralized traffic control, two-way radios and Rapidos.

Canadian National underscored the progressive attitude of the 1960s with the unveiling of a striking new-image paint scheme and stylized corporate symbol. In a radical departure from their conservative black, green and gold dress, CN passenger cars were decked out in an outstanding black and grey paint scheme; yard engines and road switchers were redone in black, with vermilion-red ends. Cab units — the most dramatic of all — debuted with red noses and alternating black and grey speed stripes angled along their sides. The traditional CNR maple leaf crest gave way to a flowing CN "noodle" applied to everything from engines and freight equipment to coaches and cabooses.

DIESELS TAKE OVER

Press releases and 8 × 10-inch glossy publicity photos conjured up images of modern, efficient railroads on the road to the future. In the real world though, modern railroading had its dark side. The economies of dieselization exacted a severe toll from those whose livelihoods were dependent upon the labor intensity of steam operation. The diesel's ability to run further and longer without attention prompted thousands of layoffs at roundhouses and shops across the land. Dozens of division points and engine changes were eliminated — and as the coal chutes and water towers were toppled, and wrecking balls crashed through roundhouse walls, countless railroaders faced the grim prospect of being left behind as the railroads rolled into the future.

There were other victims of dieselization as well. Catenary wires strung above most of the surviving Canadian interurban lines were de-energized and diesels took over. Between 1956 and 1964, Canadian National ended electric operation on its Ontario and Quebec subsidiaries: the Quebec Railway Light and Power Co., the Niagara St. Catherines and Toronto Railway, the Montreal & Southern Counties and the Oshawa Railway. On the Preston, Ontario-headquartered CP Electric Lines (formally known as the Grand River Railway and the Lake Erie & Northern Railway), Baldwin-Westinghouse steeple-cab electrics surrendered their Waterloo–Port Dover duties to CPR diesels on October 1, 1961. Electric operations on the London & Port Stanley ended in 1965, on the eve of its purchase by the CNR.

NEW LIFE FOR THE PGE

Concurrent with the dieselization of Canadian railroads was the postwar boom in resource development in the northland — Canada's last frontier. Railroads were at the fore of this new wave of development and British Columbia's Pacific Great Eastern — a frontier road in spirit and in fact — was one of the first to capitalize on the burgeoning demand for natural resources.

The boom hit the PGE in 1949. Simultaneously, the Pacific Great Eastern began building north to Prince George and commenced dieselization — buying GE 70 Tonners and later, MLW RSC3s, RS3s, RS10s and RS18s. By the early 1950s, PGE was billing itself as the first all-diesel railway in North America (a claim disputed by the Texas–Mexican Railway) and in 1952, the "Prince George Eventually" made it. Wearing a large sign proclaiming "Hello! Prince George We're Here," a pair of Pacific Great Eastern RSC3s rolled the first PGE train into Prince George on October 31, 1952.

Canadian National opened the 1960s with the introduction of a striking new paint scheme early in 1961. Cab units got the most dramatic treatment, with bold vermillion-red noses and alternating black and white stripes along their sides. CN F7A No. 9126 shows off new paint in the Calder Yard diesel shop at Edmonton, Alberta. *James A. Brown*

RESOURCE RAILWAYS

For the newly revitalized PGE, Prince George was just the beginning. In 1956, the long-overdue Squamish–North Vancouver line was completed, and by the close of the decade, the PGE had been extended over 200 miles beyond Prince George, into the Peace River District. The new northern terminus of the PGE was Fort St. John, B.C. and a branch running east from Chetwynd (on the Fort St. John line, 194 miles north of Prince George) to Dawson Creek, B.C. established a connection with the Northern Alberta Railways. In a single decade, the PGE had more than doubled in size and its traffic had mushroomed from 9,080 cars handled in 1949 to more than 60,000 in 1959.

From an often satirized railroad running from "nowhere to nowhere," the PGE graduated to a flourishing resource road, boasting piggyback service, RDCs, microwave-relayed radio dispatching and diesels. However, technological improvements could not tame the PGE's turf, where sustained 2.2 percent gradients are the norm, where rock slides pose an ever-present threat and a 60–80 car train powered by five four-axle MLW hoods could require up to 16 hours to make the trip.

One of Canada's earliest single-commodity resource railroads was the 357-mile Quebec North Shore & Labrador, opened in 1954, between the north shore St. Lawrence River port of Sept Iles, Quebec and the extensive Labrador/Quebec iron ore ranges at Schefferville. In 1960, the Iron Ore Company of Canada built the Wabush Lake Railway, running east from the QNS&L at Ross Bay Jct. (224 miles north of Sept Iles) to mines at Labrador City and Wabush Lake, Labrador. In conjunction with this project, the Arnaud Railway was built from the QNS&L at Arnaud Jct. (just north of Sept Iles) and the St. Lawrence port of Pointe Noir. Wabush/Arnaud ore traffic is routed over the QNS&L between Ross Bay Jct. and Arnaud Jct.

Forty miles upstream from the QNS&L, the Cartier Railway struck north from Port Cartier, Quebec to iron ore mines at Lac Jeannine, Quebec. The 193-mile line was opened in 1960 and extended further north to Mount Wright in the early 1970s.

While the QNS&L has relied almost entirely upon GMD road power — from GP7s and GP9s

Top Left: A GP9 in the old green-and-gold colours is tucked behind an A-B-A of GMD cabs on the Super Continental at Jasper, Alberta on May 16, 1964. *R. J. Sandusky*

Left Centre: Thirty-two months before the catenary came down, Lake Erie & Northern steeple-cab electric No. 335 switches under the wires at Galt, Ont. on February 21, 1959. *Jim Shaughnessy*

Centre: Owned by the City of London, Ontario, the London & Port Stanley did not dieselize until just before its January 1, 1966 sale to the CNR. Pantograph-equipped freight motor L2 works at St. Thomas, Ont. on September 2, 1954. *J. Chesen/David M. More Collection*

Left: In contrast to the Tumbler Ridge Branch, ancient but active 1914-built ex-Canadian Northern boxcab electrics continue to work out of Montreal as they have for more than 70 years. Seventy-year-old CN boxcab No. 6711 pauses at Val Royal, Que. with a five-car train of heavyweight coaches on March 16, 1984. *Greg McDonnell*

Top: Low-nose RS18 No. 614 leads RS10 No. 582 and RS3 No. 574 in a typically all-MLW PGE consist north of Vancouver, B.C. in 1965. *L. N. Herbert*

Bottom Left: On October 31, 1952, the "Prince George Eventually" finally made it. Wearing a sign proclaiming "Hello! Prince George We're Here," a pair of Pacific Great Eastern RSC3's prepare to leave Squamish with the inaugural train to Prince George, B.C., establishing the PGE's first physical connection with an outside railroad — Canadian National's ex-Grand Trunk Pacific mainline to Prince Rupert, B.C. Within several years, the 567 and her sister MLW-built RSC3's will lose their distinctive "boiler-tube" pilots and trade their six-axle A1A trucks for standard B-B's. *Peter Cox*

Bottom: **Although mine shutdowns have slowed traffic on the Quebec North Shore & Labrador to a trickle, the road continues to provide passenger service to remote points in the interior of Labrador and Quebec. In better times, QNS&L SD40-2 No. 257 leads the first section of the Sunday evening train on the 358-mile, Sept Iles–Schefferville, Quebec passenger run.** *Greg McDonnell*

to SD40–2s — its north shore companions have been traditional Alco/MLW strongholds. Since its inception, the Wabush/Arnaud has been staffed by MLW RS18s and with the exception of nine GP9s, the 281-mile Cartier is all-Alco/MLW as well, with a roster ranging from low-nose RS18s to six-axle DL600Bs, C630s, C636s and M636s.

Still further west, the 55-mile Roberval & Saguenay, running between Port Alfred (on the Saguenay River) and Kenogami, Quebec, is another Alco/MLW preserve. Incorporated as the Ha! Ha! Bay Railway in 1911, the R&S has since become the property of the Aluminium Company of Canada. Rostering a small fleet of four-axle Alcos and MLWs (from RS18s and M420TRs to hand-me-down C420s), the R&S now exists primarily to serve the sprawling Alcan facilities at Arvida and expends considerable energy hauling bauxite from Port Alfred to Arvida.

During the early 1950s, construction of several hundred miles of new CNR branchlines probing the mineral-rich regions of northern Quebec and Manitoba heralded a new wave of expansion that would ultimately see the first rails spiked into the North West Territories. Renewed interest in the north was manifested in 1953, with the opening of the 144-mile Lynn Lake Extension in Manitoba and the completion of over 350 miles of new lines in northern Quebec between 1953 and 1954. During the same period, several shorter resource branches were opened in northern Ontario, British Columbia and New Brunswick. By 1960, northern Manitoba mileage had been further expanded with the construction of a 31-mile branch from the Churchill line into Thompson and a 59-mile branch extending east from the Lynn Lake line into Osborne Lake.

Top: While new lines and new interests probed the far north, it was business as usual on the White Pass & Yukon — the north's own railroad. The WP&Y dieselized with custom-built, Alco-powered, shovel-nosed GE cabs and later acquired narrow-gauge Alco/MLW DL535's. Alco 251-powered GE cabs 100 and 97 prepare to leave Whithorse, Y.T. with a freight for Skagway, Alaska on June 9, 1980. *John Sutherland*

Centre: U.S. Steel's 281-mile Cartier Railway is an Alco stronghold. In June 1981, a pair of Montreal-built M636's roll a 150-car train of iron ore toward port facilities at Port Cartier, Quebec. *Greg McDonnell*

Bottom: Alcan-owned Roberval & Saguenay thrives upon bauxite traffic hauled from the docks at Port Alfred to Alcan's aluminium plant at Arvida, Que. On May 21, 1972, R&S RS18 No. 24 and M420TR No. 27 team up to return a train of empties to Port Alfred. *David M. More*

One year after CN took over the Northern Alberta Railways, four ex-NAR GMD1's work freight #884 through Fedorah, Alberta. Although all four engines in this January 27, 1982 photo have been renumbered into CN's 1000 series, only the 1082, ex-NAR 305, has been repainted. *F. D. Shaw*

Right: One of CN's five highly touted, but ill-fated, United Aircraft/MLW Turbo Trains whips through Scarborough, Ont. en route to Montreal with train #62. *David M. More*

THE GREAT SLAVE LAKE RAILWAY

The volume of new construction surged again in the early 1960s, with a flurry of activity in the mining regions of Quebec, Ontario, New Brunswick, Saskatchewan and Alberta. The most significant undertaking was CN's Great Slave Lake Railway. Sponsored by the Province of Alberta, the 377-mile Great Slave Lake Railway struck north from the Northern Alberta Railways at Roma, Alberta to tap extensive mineral deposits at Pine Point, North West Territories and to touch the shores of Great Slave Lake at Hay River, N.W.T.

The railroad crossed into the North West Territories in October, 1964, establishing the GSLR as the first, and so far, only railroad in the N.W.T. The following year, CNR GP9s, some painted in a special GSLR/CN paint scheme, were hauling trainloads of lead and zinc concentrates out of Pine Point, N.W.T. Operation of the GSLR as a separate entity was short-lived — as was the yellow livery of assigned engines and cars. In 1969, the Great Slave Lake became the Manning, Meander River and Pine Point Subdivisions of CN's Alberta North Division.

EXPANSION IN ALBERTA

Following the completion of the Great Slave Lake Railway, CN and the Alberta govern-

The Canadian Transport Commission forced a reluctant CPR to maintain a skeletal nationwide passenger network. On the Dominion Atlantic, service was provided by DAR-lettered RDC's such as RDC1 No. 9059 stopped here at Kentville, N.S. on its 217-mile Halifax–Yarmouth, N.S. run. *Jim Shaughnessy*

Centre: Pushing coupler-deep snow, CP FP7 No. 4066 and RS10 No. 8560 crawl into Montreal West, Que. with the "Atlantic Limited" from St. John, N.B. *Greg McDonnell*

Bottom: Throughout the 1960s, Canadian Pacific passenger services dwindled to a bare minimum. Symbolic of the decline, two-car Moose Jaw–North Portal, Sask. train #202 (with GP9 No. 8807) meets Work Extra 8501 north of Weyburn, Saskatchewan on August 1, 1960. *R. J. Sandusky*

ment cooperated on another resource railroad — the aptly named, provincially owned/CN operated Alberta Resources Railway. The 233-mile Swan Landing–Grande Prairie, Alberta line (built to open up vast timber and coal reserves in western Alberta) was officially opened on May 28, 1969, with the driving of a chrome-plated spike at Grande Prairie.

While the GSLR and the ARR involved extensive construction in Alberta, Canadian National's most recent expansion in the province was completed with the stroke of a pen. On January 1, 1981 — after purchasing CP's

share of the railroad — CN assumed full control of the Northern Alberta Railways, ending almost 52 years of unique, joint CN/CP ownership.

Dissolution of the CN/CP partnership on the NAR was predated by the 1965 cancellation of a more visible joint operation in the east. Effective October 31, 1965, pooled passenger services (inaugurated on April 2, 1933) in the Quebec City–Montreal–Ottawa–Toronto corridor were discontinued. In place of the Quebec–Montreal,

Montreal–Toronto and Toronto–Ottawa Pool Trains, each road implemented independent trains.

After the divorce, CP barely maintained the status quo and indeed exited the Montreal–Toronto market within a year. Conversely, CN pulled all the stops and plunged headlong — in a season when most railroads were posting more train-off notices than travel posters — into a vigorous program to revitalize long-distance and corridor passenger services nationwide.

COMMITMENT TO PASSENGER TRAINS

CN's renewed commitment to the passenger train was accented by aggressive marketing — "Red White and Blue" discount fares, upgraded equipment, faster schedules and a progressive attitude toward the passenger business. In the Quebec City–Windsor/Sarnia, Ontario corridor, well-publicized and often sold out Rapidos posted the fastest-ever Toronto–Montreal schedules. Highly touted — but ill-fated — TurboTrains were ordered to provide even faster service between the two cities and new Tempo equipment was purchased for selected Toronto–Windsor/Sarnia trains.

For the long-distance and overnight trade, CN gobbled up scores of sleepers, domes and observation cars rendered surplus as U.S. roads bailed out of the passenger business. While CPR shops converted retired sleepers and diners into work cars, surplus CP coaches headed south to Mexico. CN shops were busy refurbishing stainless-steel, ex-Reading Crusader equipment, fleets of ex-Erie, NYC, NKP, B&Mr, Frisco, BAR and FEC sleepers and former Milwaukee Road Skytop observations and full-length domes for service on re-equipped CN trains from Nova Scotia to British Columbia.

Throughout the 1960s, CP's passenger train abandonment petitions read like the system timetable. In an admitted bid to purge itself of all passenger trains, the company successfully axed scores of local and intermediate-distance trains, and even the transcontinental "Dominion" was discontinued. The Montreal/Toronto–Vancouver "Canadian" — once the pride of the fleet — produced enough red ink to cover more than the tuscan-red letterboards of its stainless-steel Budd consist. But repeated efforts to cut the train were rebuffed by the industry-governing Canadian Transport Commission. In addition, the CTC forced a reluctant CPR to maintain a skeletal nation-

Centre: Under the trainshed at Toronto Union Station, CN Passenger Extra 6530 East and train #54, with FPA4 No. 6784 and F9B No. 6634 prepare for afternoon departure to Montreal. *Greg McDonnell*

Centre Right: Like CP, CN favoured the C424 over the competition's second-generation Geeps. During 1964–1967, CN purchased two GP35's and 16 GP40's versus 41 C424's. CN's first C424, No. 3200 leads a sister into Hamilton, Ont. in February 1968. *Charles Begg*

Bottom: CN beefed up its southern Ontario corridor services with the introduction of "Tempo" trains in 1967. Assigned to selected Toronto–Windsor and Toronto–Sarnia trains, the Tempos featured rebuilt, high-speed RS18's and brand-new, electrically heated Hawker-Siddeley passenger cars. Five-car Tempo #74 drifts down Dundas Hill behind rebuilt RS18 No. 3150 on May 22, 1982. *Greg McDonnell*

Canadian Locomotive Co. exited the domestic market with a whimper. The last CLC's built for a Canadian railroad were 14 44-ton, Davenport-design diesel-hydraulic switchers built for CP between 1957 and 1960. Last of the domestic CLC's, CP No. 23 — outshopped from Kingston on May 30, 1960 — switches at Vallee Jct., Quebec on the Quebec Central. *Jim Shaughnessy*

Centre: MLW was still in good standing with Canadian Pacific in the early second-generation years and as a result, CP purchased more than twice as many MLW C424's as it did GMD GP35's. Three of 51 CPR C424's, along with an RS3 and an RS23, kick up snow as they race Extra 4218 West through Dorval, Que. in December 1969. *Greg McDonnell*

Bottom: After purchasing the only two Canadian-built GP30's, Canadian Pacific returned to GMD with orders for two dozen GP35's delivered between May 1964 and January 1966. Brand-new GP35 No. 8204 (later renumbered 5004) posed for a builder's portrait outside GMD's London plant in May 1964. *General Motors Diesel*

145

Bottom: In one of the more unusual transactions, CP leased all six Illinois Central C636's during 1970. Although the big 1100's spent most of their time out of service at St. Luc, proof that they did get out on the road can be found in this prize shot of CP #904 with IC 1105 and 1101 meeting CP Extra 8772 West (with IC 1100 trailing) at Lobo, Ont. on March 2, 1970. *James A. Brown*

146

wide passenger network.

Meanwhile, CN's ambitious efforts to revive the passenger train succeeded in reversing the decline in ridership on all but the most hopeless trains (the government road was not without its own train-off petitions). But Red White and Blue days, Rapidos, Tempos and reconditioned equipment could not stem rising passenger train deficits. As a result, government was destined to play an increasing role in the operation of Canadian passenger trains.

SECOND GENERATION DIESELS

Canadian railroads had barely accomplished dieselizing when U.S. locomotive builders began encouraging railroads south of the border to trade in their FTs, early Es, vintage Alcos and products of minority builders for second-generation diesels. In a country that had built new steam through the entire production years of the FT, FTs and early Es, vintage Alcos and products of minority builders were rare to nonexistant. As a result, Canadian locomotive builders received precious few orders during the early 1960s.

For the Canadian Locomotive Company, the drought in domestic diesel orders was permanent. CLC delivered its last major Canadian order — five CPR 44-ton, Davenport-design diesel hydraulic switchers — in May, 1960, subsisted on meagre export business for several years and finally closed for good in early 1968.

Second-generation diesels finally debuted in Canada in 1963, when Canadian Pacific took delivery of a pair of GMD GP30s and a single MLW C424. CN's initial second-generation purchases were made the following year, with two GP35s coming from GMD and two C424s from MLW. Both roads took a conservative approach to redieselization, observing the

Top Left: The cowl-nosed "safety cab" developed by CN in the early 1970s has been a standard feature on all CN power delivered since 1973. Three cowl-nosed GP40-2L's grind upgrade through Bayview Jct. in Hamilton, Ont., with Niagara Falls–Toronto freight #436 on August 19, 1983. *Greg McDonnell* The distinctive cab has been applied to GP38-2's, GP40-2L's, SD40-2's as well as MLW/ Bombardier (in a cosmetically different version) M420's, HR412's and full-cowl HR616's.

Top Centre: During the power shortages of the 1960s and 1970s, Bessemer & Lake Erie F7's were perennial favourites with both CN and CP. Freshly painted B&LE F7A No. 713 leads CP RS10 No. 8598 on an Extra West at Lisgar, Ont. on December 26, 1965. *James A. Brown*

Centre: Canadian Pacific purchased its first SD40, No. 5500, in July 1966 as part of an order for 32 units. A brief infatuation with six-motor MLW M630's and M636's interrupted SD40 acquisitions, but purchases of the C-C GM's resumed in 1972 and by 1985, CP Rail rostered 569 SD40/ SD40-2's. Eastbound at Seebee, Alberta on March 1, 1980, are four of CP's favourite diesels: SD40-2's Nos. 5858, 5654, 5610 and 5576. *F. D. Shaw*

Bottom Left: In 1972, CP's appetite for SD40-2's exceeded the production capabilities of GM's London plant. To satisfy immediate power requirements, 30 CP Rail SD40-2's were built by EMD at La Grange, Illinois and delivered to CP during November and December 1972. U.S.-built SD40-2 No. 5656 leads Canadian-built No. 5603 and begrimed tuscan-and-grey MLW No. C630 past a derailment at Brant, Alberta on April 23, 1974. *Andrew J. Sutherland*

Right: A quartet of the engines that soured the relationship between CP and MLW work Extra 4730 West upgrade through Guelph Jct., Ont., on July 6, 1981. Trailing M636 No. 4730 are sisters Nos. 4721, 4742 and M630 4551. *Greg McDonnell*

Top: A matched set of 20-year-old F's, FP9A No. 1406 and F9B No. 4477 exit the Lower Spiral Tunnel with CP #2, the "Canadian," in March 1974. *W. R. Hooper*

Right: A Baldwin bailiwick since it was dieselized in 1949, CP's Vancouver Island subsidiary Esquimalt & Nanaimo became one of the continent's last bastions of Baldwin roadswitchers. A year away from retirement, CP DRS4-4-1000's Nos. 8000 and 8002 probe weed-choked E&N trackage at Lake Cowichan, B.C. on June 12, 1974. *Andrew J. Sutherland*

Left: Flood waters reflect CP H16-44 No. 8728 northbound at Wasa, B.C. on CP's CLC-stronghold, the southern B.C. "Kootenay Division." *Greg McDonnell*

Bottom: Illuminated by a half-dozen synchronized Type 2 flashbulbs, standard-cab SD40 No. 5034 leads cowl-nosed GP40-2L No. 9520 and full-cowl HR616 No. 2116 through Dundas, Ont. with #411 at 01:58, March 15, 1983. *Greg McDonnell*

performance of the new units for at least a year before submitting repeat orders. Despite satisfaction with the products of both builders and subsequent orders (CN for 39 C424s and 16 GP40s, CP for 24 GP35s and 50 C424s), mass redieselization was several years away.

A mid-1960s upswing in traffic terminated plans to trade in aging road units on new diesels — but not before early trades claimed a number of older CNR MLWs and decimated the ranks of CP's original Alco FA fleet (the majority of CP's MLW cabs survived, though). Recurring power shortages secured the immediate future of elderly engines that had previously been eyed as prospective trade-in material. Aging FAs worked mainline power pools with brand-new C424s and leased power — as exotic as Union Pacific FAs on CP and as unlikely as Chicago & Western Indiana RS1s and Bessemer & Lake Erie F7s on CN and CP — bolstered CN and CP fleets during the most severe shortages.

Redieselization became a gradual — and in fact ongoing — process and the transitional period proved to be one of Canadian railroading's most colorful phases. While the first-generation diesel made a spectacular last stand, Canadian motive power philosophies did an about-face, abandoning the traditional preference for smaller power and embracing six-motor diesels with unprecedented enthusiasm. The General Motors SD40 and its Dash 2 successor, the SD40-2, became the most popular and successful diesel locomotives in Canadian history. Meanwhile MLW was nearly driven out of the diesel business after producing the infamous M-line derivatives of the Alco Century line. Canadian Pacific embarked on a 1968, company-wide image overhaul, from which the railway emerged — minus its traditional tuscan-and-grey colors and beaver crest — as "action" red multimarked "CP Rail" and in the same period, Pacific Great Eastern became the British Columbia Railway. Canadian National took the diesel locomotive cab back to the drawing board, developing a cowl-nosed safety cab that

would become the hallmark of post-1973 CN power.

By the early 1970s, second-generation diesels were taking over. CN's entire CLC fleet and most 244-engined CNR MLWs were retired; CP had junked two-thirds of its Train Masters and was buying SD40s almost as fast as London could build them. However, with bastions of first-generation power holding down assignments from coast to coast, Canada became one of the last preserves of an endangered species. While London outshopped hundreds of SD40/SD40–2s, GP40–2Ls and GP38–2s, and MLW filled token domestic orders, aging GE 70 Tonners worked CNR branchlines on Prince Edward Island and 539-

engined RSC13s held down wayfreight assignments on mainland Maritime branches. Canadian Pacific squeezed every last bit of life out of battered RS3s, RS10s and FAs. Its Nelson, B.C.-based Kootenay Division was staffed with rare CLC-FM H16–44s, H24–66s and the last surviving C-line cabs anywhere. The Vancouver Island Esquimault & Naniamo subsidiary operated with the same Baldwin DRS–4–4 1000s that had dieselized the island railroad in 1949. CN and CP regularly dispatched transcontinental passenger trains behind matched A–B–A sets of GMD cabs and seemingly ageless MLW FPA4s could still top 90-plus miles per hour wheeling CN passenger trains in the Ontario–Quebec corridor. GP9s were still regarded as staple power; GMD1s ruled CN's prairie branchlines and durable 539-engined Alco/MLW switchers worked in yards from Atlantic to Pacific.

As the decade progressed, SD40s and second-generation Geeps toppled most of the remaining first-generation strongholds. Baldwins and CLCs were exterminated, 244-powered MLWs became increasingly rare and retrucked RS18s forced CN's 70 Tonners and RSC13s into retirement. First generation survivors of the turbulent decade included venerable Alco/ MLW switchers dating back to World War II, infatigable GP9s and GMD1s, RS18s — surely the best diesels MLW ever built — GMD F-units and CNs remarkable FPA4s — the last active Alco cabs north of Mexico.

THE RISE OF VIA

To the average Canadian, the decline of the first-generation diesel and the resultant rise of the SD40 mattered naught, but during the 1970s, the future of the country's passenger trains became a federal election issue. Passenger train losses were mounting and ridership outside the populated corridors was plummeting. Government response to the increasingly urgent situation was overdue: Canada was the last major country in the world to ignore the federal responsibility for the operation of the intercity passenger train.

During the 1974 election campaign, Prime Minister Pierre Trudeau addressed the situation with the promise of a Crown Corporation to assume funding and operation of the nation's passenger trains and to improve service in the Quebec–Ontario corridor. Trudeau's Liberal Party was returned to power. Out of his 1974 campaign promise rose VIA Rail Canada, a Crown Corporation responsible for the intercity passenger operations of CN and CP Rail.

Unlike Amtrak's overnight takeover of passenger service in the U.S., VIA came on the scene gradually. VIA colors first appeared on a CN TurboTrain in the spring of 1976. Thereafter, CN passenger locomotives and equipment began to emerge from the paint shops in blue and yellow VIA/CN colors.

VIA Rail Canada acquired formal status as a Crown Corporation in January, 1977 and began marketing CN/CP passenger services in June of that year. On April 1, 1978, the Crown Corporation took title to CN's passenger locomotives and cars and assumed full responsibility of the railroad's intercity passenger operations. VIA struck a similar agreement with CP Rail six months later. On October 29, 1978, the promised national passenger railroad was complete. Excluded from VIA were CN and CP commuter trains and passenger trains operated by Algoma Central, Ontario Northland, Quebec North Shore and Labrador, Northern Alberta, the British Columbia Railway and CNR mixed trains operating in Newfoundland. The latter remained the responsibility of CN's recently formed Newfoundland subsidiary, Terra Transport.

VIA inherited a Halifax to Victoria system of 15,389 route-miles, serviced by 157 trains as disparate as remote northland mixed trains and 100 mph-plus Turbos. Equipment was as old as heavyweight ex-CN parlour cars built in 1920 and as new as lightweight 1968-vintage Tempo equipment. Locomotives were primarily ex-CN and CP GMD F-units and former CNR FPA/FPB4s, although the corporation also acquired an ex-CP RS10 and the two surviving CPR E8s. In addition, VIA continued to lease CN GP9s and RS18s, along with steam generator-equipped CPR GP9s and RS10s.

Under the circumstances, VIA functioned well from the start, but transcontinental services — the ex-CP *Canadian* and the former CN *Super Continental* — were gobbling up enormous portions of VIA funds. The equipment was suffering from old age and on the Quebec–Ontario corridor, elderly diesels and equipment were being pushed to the limit — moving more than two-thirds of VIA's more than 6.5 million annual riders.

Fully aware that more than blue and yellow paint would be necessary to rebuild the nation's rail-passenger services, VIA took immediate action. Bombardier (formerly MLW) LRC — "Light Rapid Comfortable" — train sets were ordered for corridor services; locomotives and cars were shopped, schedules improved and to ease the financial drain, money-losing nonessential services were dropped. In spite of cuts on several routes, VIA ridership grew by a staggering 41 percent in the first five years.

Despite its best intentions, VIA soon fell on hard times. In the fall of 1981, a nationwide

hue and cry was raised as a severe, federally mandated budget cut forced VIA — in spite of the 41 percent increase in ridership — to axe well-patronized trains. Included were the often sold-out Super Continental, the popular Montreal–St. John, New Brunswick–Halifax Nova Scotia "Atlantic" and a host of lesser trains, some of which constituted the only public transportation to remote localities.

To make matters worse, the Bombardier LRCs — upon which VIA had placed such high hopes — were plagued with serious break-in problems. The first new trains arrived on the property in the summer of 1981, but mechanical difficulties with the 3725-hp, Alco-design 251-engined LRC diesels, as well as the aluminium Bombardier-built coaches, delayed the start of revenue LRC runs until 1982.

While Bombardier and VIA struggled to make the new trains perform, VIA took delivery of enough cars to form ten train sets, as well as 31 engines — a quantity sufficient to work with all of the LRC cars and supply an additional ten LRC locomotives for use with conventional cars. The LRC diesels can MU with regular locomotives, heat and supply power to Tempo equipment and, with the addition of a steam generator car, work trains with standard, steam-heated cars.

LRCs became a common sight on the corridor as bugs were worked out and the equipment became workable. However, it had become all too apparent that the LRC was not the saviour that VIA had sought and the corporation searched for a new solution to its equipment woes. An Amtrak EMD F40PH and bilevel Superliner cars were leased for testing on the Winnipeg–Edmonton "Panorama" during the winter of 1985 and Ontario Northland's order for double-deck equipment similar to that in use by Toronto's GO Transit was studied carefully.

VIA found a friend in Ottawa after the 1984 federal election put the progressive Conservatives in power with a landslide victory. The Tories made good an election promise to restore most of the trains axed in the 1981 cuts. In June 1985, the Atlantic, the Super Continental and some of the less prestigious victims of 1981 rolled again.

Though still beset with equipment shortages and the frailties of aging locomotives and rolling stock, VIA is fulfilling its mandate as the nation's passenger railroad. Seven days a week, rugged MLW FPA4s — closing in on 30 years of age — hustle corridor trains along at speeds in excess of 90 miles per hour and in the grand tradition, often assemble in A-B-A or A-B-B formation to work 15- to 20-car, Montreal–Halifax trains. RDCs skirt the shores of the Bay of Fundy on CP's Dominion Atlantic Railway and probe the spectacular interior of Vancouver Island on the Esquimault and

Centre: No major Canadian railroad has remained as loyal to MLW as the British Columbia Railway (formerly the PGE). The provincially owned road bought only MLW power for decades, received its first GM diesels (SD40-2's) in 1980 and continues to field a predominantly MLW roster. In typically rugged BCR territory, a trio of BCR M630's enter the Cheakamus River Canyon with Extra 717 South in June 1981. *Dale Sanders*

Centre Bottom Left: VIA colours first appeared on a CN TurboTrain in the spring of 1976. Four years later, a blue-and-yellow Turbo glides through Newtonnville, Ont., with VIA #66 on June 16, 1980. *Greg McDonnell*

Bottom: Excluded from VIA, British Columbia Railway #2, with RDC3 BC30, overtakes southbound BCR freight #32 at Alexandria, B.C. on September 25, 1979. *Philip R. Hastings*

Nanaimo. Blue-and-yellow VIA trains call on remote terminals at Prince Rupert, B.C., Churchill, Manitoba, and Chicoutimi, Quebec. You can still board a sleeping car in Toronto and wake up on the outskirts of Montreal early the next morning. And, thanks to cooperation between Amtrak and VIA, you can walk aboard an Amtrak train in Chicago's Union Station or New York's Grand Central and detrain at Toronto Union Station.

Last, but certainly not least, the "Canadian," the celebrated VIA flagship, departs daily from Vancouver and from Toronto on its four-night/three-day transcontinental journey. With matched sets of F-units drawing impressive consists of glistening stainless-steel, ex-CPR Budd-built equipment, punctuated by a smattering of former CN cars in VIA blue and properly trailing a stainless-steel, Park series dome-observation (sporting a lighted VIA drumhead, of course), the "Canadian" is the pride of the fleet. Its cars and locomotives may be aged (the Fs are pure first generation and the stainless-steel Budd equipment dates from the original 1955 CPR "Canadian"), but as the "Canadian" flashes through the desolate northern Ontario shield country, slides gracefully across the prairies and coils majestically through the mountain ranges of British Columbia, it is the personification of VIA's national mandate and no less than a blue, black, yellow and silver symbol of national unity.

PRAIRIE RECONSTRUCTION

The Liberals may have been brutal with VIA, but in the west, where the Crow Rate was strangling the railroads, Trudeau's govern-

ment sponsored the massive Prairie Branch Line Rehabilitation Program. In November, 1983, the Crows Nest Pass Agreement was finally abolished with the passage of Bill C-155, the Western Grain Transportation Act. The combined effect of these moves opened a new season of railroad construction and reconstruction throughout western Canada, on a scale unseen since steel was first stretched across the west.

On the prairies, branchline rehabilitation costs soared above $1 billion, as ballast gangs, steel gangs, bridge crews, heavy machinery and work trains rebuilt thousands of miles of branchlines from the substructure up. New ballast was laid, ties replaced, bridges rebuilt, drainage improved, banks widened and heavier rail installed. When the work gangs and machinery moved on, branches that had posted turn-of-the-century speed and weight restrictions, included rail as light as 65 pounds to the yard, and were often limited to light-weight diesels and 50-foot boxcars, were finally capable of handling Geeps and 100-ton hoppers.

The cost and scope of the prairie reconstruction was eclipsed by projects underway in British Columbia. Canadian National embarked upon extensive upgrading and limited double-tracking of its mountain mainlines, boosting the efficiency and capacity of the railroad. As part of the program, the former Grand Trunk Pacific main to Prince Rupert, long the exclusive domain of four-axle power, primarily Geeps and F-units, was upgraded. The program included laying concrete ties and 152-pound welded rail, rebuilding bridges, extending sidings and adding new ones, all to handle multiple SD40 lashups and unit grain and coal trains on the old GTP.

The entire prairie rehab program and CN's mainline rebuilding combined pale in comparison to CP Rail's mountain mainline mega-projects. In the largest undertaking since the construction of the transcontinental railway, Canadian Pacific unveiled, in 1981, plans to increase its mainline capacity through the mountains with a ten-year, $7.6-billion capital

Top: Closing in on 30 years of age, VIA's never-say-die MLW FPA4's continue to hustle corridor trains along at speeds in excess of 90 m.p.h., seven days a week. Spliced by F9B No. 6627, VIA FPA4 No. 6784 and FPB4 No. 6868 lift Montreal–Toronto #53 out of Brockville, Ont. on June 6, 1981. *Greg McDonnell*

Top Centre: Bombardier-built LRC No. 6904 trails a steam generator car and two standard coaches through Paris, Ontario on Sarnia–Toronto #86 on January 17, 1983. *Greg McDonnell*

Centre: On one of VIA's most spectacular runs, ex-CN FP9 No. 6514 leads the Prince Rupert–Jasper "Skeena" into Terrace, B.C. in June 1983. *Dale Sanders*

Left: Also left out of VIA were CN's Newfoundland mixed trains, operated by CN subsidiary Terra Transport. Homeward-bound Bonavista Mixed crosses the northwest arm of Trinity Bay with only an empty hopper separating G8 No. 804 and the coach. Newfoundland mixed trains have since been reduced to a single train on the mainline between Bishops Falls and Cornerbrook. *R. J. Sandusky*

program. Equipment expenditures, localized double-tracking and grade reduction plans are included in the figure and the program is highlighted by the $600 million Rogers Pass Project.

In the works since 1972, the Rogers Pass Project involves construction of a new double-track bypass around — and in fact under — one of the system's most serious bottlenecks, the westbound assault on the east slope of the Selkirk Mountains between Golden and Revelstoke, B.C. The major task in double-tracking the Selkirk line and reducing the westbound ascent to an average 1 percent is the construction of two tunnels — a one-mile bore beneath the Trans-Canada Highway and a 9.11-mile tunnel, 325 feet lower than the present Connaught Tunnel and 840 feet below the summit of Rogers Pass.

The nine-mile tunnel will include automatically opened doors on the east portal and at midtunnel to control ventilation. An 11,250 horsepower ventilation system (that's more horsepower than three SD40s) will force fresh air through vent shafts and along the length of passing trains — cooling locomotives and driving exhaust fumes from the bore. Electrification has been considered and the tunnel clearances allow for potential installation of 50kV overhead catenary.

In the 1980s, railroading offers few spectacles more overwhelming than the sight, sound and smell of no less than 12 screaming SD40s (four on the head end, three remote-control midtrain helpers and five pushers) exiting the Beaver River Valley with grain trains and 14,000-ton, 108-car coal trains stretched out on the 2.6 percent ruling grade.

Completion of the tunnels and new Rogers Pass line is targeted for the end of the decade. When the project is finished, CP Rail will be capable of shoving extra trains and increased tonnage through the mountains, pusher service will be eliminated, Rogers Pass will be crested several hundred feet underground and the Selkirks will never be the same.

THE BRITISH COLUMBIA RAILWAY

Several hundred miles northwest of Rogers Pass, deep in the B.C. interior, the British Columbia Railway is operating Canada's newest railroad. Opened in December, 1983, BCR's 80-mile, $447-million Tumbler Ridge branch extends east from the BCR mainline at Ansac (48 miles north of Prince George) to the Tumbler Ridge coal fields. Built through some of the most rugged terrain in the country, the branch is notable not for its spectacular scenery (of which there is plenty), nor for its lengthy tunnels (one over four miles and the other just under six miles in length), but rather for the 50kV catenary strung overhead. The Tumbler Ridge branch is Canada's first electrified, heavy-duty freight railroad and only the third in the world to utilize a 50kV power supply.

Tumbler Ridge motive power is notable too. Built at the General Motors Diesel Division plant at London, Ont., BCR's seven 6000 hp, C-C, GF6C electrics (numbered 6001–6007) are the first challengers of Canadian dieselization and could be harbingers of the next generation of mainline power — at least in the Canadian west. CP Rail, consultant on the Tumbler Ridge rail line, has not ruled out electrification of its mountain mainline. One of the justifications for electrifying the Tumbler Ridge line was the immense cost of tunnel ventilation — a criteria

that is certainly applicable to the Rogers Pass project now underway. CP's Rogers Pass tunnels will have clearances large enough to accommodate catenary and although there are no immediate plans to do so, the precedent has been set and the technology is ready and waiting.

With extended pantographs drawing life-giving 50,000-volt AC current from overhead catenary, red-white-and-blue British Columbia Railway GF6Cs roll 98-car, 10,000-ton–plus coal trains from Tumbler Ridge to Ansac, where pooled BCR/CNR diesels take over to move export coal — bound for Japanese steel mills — to the ocean terminal at Prince Rupert, B.C.

The Tumbler Ridge branch is BCR's showcase and the epitome of frontier railroading — 1980s style. Railway builders surveyed, graded, spiked, bridged and bored the line to Tumbler Ridge through country as wild and as uncivilized as that confronting Andrew Onderdonk's crews a full century earlier. Although the distance involved was fractional and the technology improved a hundred-fold over that available to Onderdonk and his men, the challenge facing the builders of the Tumbler Ridge branch was similar and the frontier spirit proved to be unchanged over a hundred years.

THE FUTURE AND THE PAST

If indeed the future of Canadian railroading is to be found in the remote wilds of British Columbia, its past is never further away than the nearest railroad — mainline, branchline, or otherwise. Canada's railroad heritage is a tangible element of everyday railroading — in fact everyday life — from Prince Rupert, B.C. — where the Grand Trunk Pacific dreams of establishing the "Halifax of the west" are only now becoming a reality, as braces of CN SD40s roll in from the east with increasing coal and export grain tonnage — to St. John's, Newfoundland — where NEWFOUNDLAND RAILWAY is still emblazoned across the cornice of the CN/Terra Transport locomotive shops and the distance between the rails of the transinsular railway measures 42 inches, as it has since 1881. It is a heritage that lives on in the ancient — but active — 1914-built, ex-Canadian Northern boxcab electrics that have been grinding through the Mount Royal Tunnel for more than 70 years and in the 1882-vintage, ex-CPR 4–4–0 annually revived for summer-long excursion service out of Winnipeg. It is as obvious as the architecture of former Grand Trunk stations in the east and as subtle as the knowledge that the precarious rock ledge that carries 14,000-ton CPR grain trains through the Fraser River Canyon was carved into the sheer rock walls by Andrew Onderdonk's railroad builders over a century ago. The history of Canadian railroads is not just locked in the nation's archives, museums and libraries. It is an integral and visible ingredient of today's railroading. The key to discovering it is as simple as the message stencilled on the antiquated wigwag crossing signals that continue to guard a handful of the country's railway crossings — "Stop, Look and Listen."

Top: One of only 16 CN GP40's, No. 4004 leads a leased C&O GP9 and a CN SD40 through Aldershot, Ont. on September 8, 1973. Although CN all but ignored the GP40 — buying C424's instead — the government road began purchasing GP40-2L's en masse in 1974 and in 17 months assembled a fleet of 233 of the 3,000 h.p., four-axle, cowl-nosed hoods, numbered 9400–9632. *F. D. Shaw*

Top Left: East of Jasper, Alberta, wide-nosed CN SD40-2 No. 5313 and standard-cab SD40's 5192 and 5059 work Vancouver-bound freight #217 through recently double-tracked territory on August 28, 1981. *F. D. Shaw*

Centre Left: Canada's newest railway is the British Columbia Railway's electrified, 80-mile, $447-million Tumbler Ridge Branch, running from the BCR mainline at Ansac to the Tumbler Ridge coal fields. Running under 50kV catenary, a quartet of BCR GF6C electrics move a 98-car coal train south of Tumbler Ridge in July 1984. *Dale Sanders*